AF557814

MODI'S **NORTH EAST** STORY

'Tuhin Sinha and Aditya Pittie have compiled an evocative account of the development and growth of the Northeast under the visionary leadership of Prime Minister Narendra Modi. It is well-known that, despite being a vital corridor of the country, brimming with abundant natural resources and extraordinary biodiversity as well as skilled and available human capital, the Northeast had been ignored for far too long under previous regimes. Thought-provoking essays from leaders and intellectuals illustrate the Modi government's holistic transformation of the region.

Underpinned by the twin pillars of peace and development, and manifested in unprecedented infrastructure creation and increase in connectivity, the Northeast is witnessing an exponential leap in its quality of life today. Stunning victories for the BJP and its partners in state Assembly elections indicate the people's broad acceptance of the *Sabka Saath, Sabka Vikas* philosophy.

Modi's Northeast Story not only captures the development journey of the Northeast but also paints a vivid portrait of the rich cultural legacy of the region itself as well as the unyielding resilience and positivity of its people. It is a laudable accomplishment. I hope that it is read widely—people should know about the scale of transformation that has been unleashed in the Northeast.'

—Hardeep S. Puri
Union Minister, Petroleum and Natural Gas &
Housing and Urban Affairs

'The sheer magnitude of all-round transformation of the Northeastern states in the last nine years under PM Narendra Modi's dynamic leadership, is a case study for all students of politics and public policy. The speed of infrastructure projects undertaken in border areas has boosted the standard of living in far-flung districts. At the same time, restoration of age-old conflicts and improved law and order situation has led to record tourist footfalls in the region. Under PM Modi's visionary leadership, the Northeast has emerged as an important reservoir for India's growth in the decades to come.'

—Devendra Fadnavis
Deputy Chief Minister of Maharashtra

MODI'S NORTH EAST STORY

With essays from

HIMANTA BISWA SARMA, KIREN RIJIJU, PEMA KHANDU

Edited by

Tuhin A. Sinha

Aditya Pittie

RUPA

Published by
Rupa Publications India Pvt. Ltd 2024
7/16, Ansari Road, Daryaganj
New Delhi 110002

Sales centres:
Bengaluru Chennai
Hyderabad Jaipur Kathmandu
Kolkata Mumbai Prayagraj

Edition and Introduction copyright © Tuhin A. Sinha and Aditya Pittie 2024
Foreword copyright © J.P. Nadda 2024

Copyright for individual pieces vests with the respective authors.

The views and opinions expressed in this book are the authors' own and the facts are as reported by them which have been verified to the extent possible, and the publishers are not in any way liable for the same.

All rights reserved.
No part of this publication may be reproduced, transmitted, or stored in a retrieval system, in any form or by any means, electronic, mechanical, photocopying, recording or otherwise, without the prior permission of the publisher.

P-ISBN: 978-93-90260-86-7
E-ISBN: 978-93-90260-98-0

First impression 2024

10 9 8 7 6 5 4 3 2 1

The moral right of the authors has been asserted.

Printed in India

This book is sold subject to the condition that it shall not, by way of trade or otherwise, be lent, resold, hired out, or otherwise circulated, without the publisher's prior consent, in any form of binding or cover other than that in which it is published.

Dedicated to the 4.7 crore people of our Northeastern states who are finally at the forefront of Bharat's resurgence.

ᔕ

CONTENTS

FOREWORD

It is with great pleasure that I extend my heartfelt appreciation for the remarkable work encapsulated within the pages of this book, *Modi's Northeast Story*. An eclectic anthology, conceived, curated and edited by Shri Tuhin A. Sinha and Shri Aditya Pittie, it meticulously captures the transformative journey of the Northeastern states of India under the dynamic leadership of Prime Minister (PM) Narendra Modi. This comprehensive work stands as a testament to the visionary leadership and unwavering commitment of our PM towards bringing about positive changes in one of the most geographically diverse and culturally rich parts of our nation.

The development initiatives executed in the Northeast under the visionary leadership of PM Modi stand as a testament to the power of dedication, foresight and a relentless pursuit of progress.

The Northeast has always been blessed with unparalleled natural beauty and cultural diversity. However, for far too long, the immense potential of this region remained untapped due to infrastructural constraints, connectivity challenges and socio-economic disparities. Recognizing the significance of harnessing this potential, PM Modi embarked on a journey to usher in a new era of growth and prosperity for the people of Northeast India.

The chapters of this book unfold the story of a transformational odyssey that encompasses infrastructural advancements, connectivity revolutions and socio-economic empowerment. The Northeast has witnessed the creation of modern highways, bridges and networks that have not only facilitated easier movement but have also catalysed economic activities and promoted cultural exchanges. The launch of the 'Act East Policy' has opened new avenues for trade, investment and collaborations, connecting the region not only to the rest of India but to the wider Asia–Pacific region.

Prime Minister Modi's unwavering commitment to the welfare of every citizen is exemplified through various initiatives focussed on healthcare, education, skill development and employment generation. This book rightly highlights how these efforts have led to a rise in living standards, increased access to quality education and enhanced healthcare facilities. The success stories of local entrepreneurs from the Northeast are a testament to the transformative impact of these initiatives.

While infrastructure and economic development are crucial, the preservation and promotion of the unique cultural heritage of the Northeast have not been overlooked. Prime Minister Modi's dedication to nurture and celebrate the diverse traditions, languages and customs of the region has not only strengthened the social fabric but has also projected the Northeast onto the global stage.

As the Bharatiya Janata Party (BJP) National President, I am very happy to note the involvement and enthusiasm of our party *karyakartas* in supporting government initiatives on the ground. Throughout the Covid-19 pandemic, our karyakartas were available in every nook and corner of the Northeast, extending help to the people in distress. In the last few years, the BJP has given credible leadership to the Northeast. Some of these youth leaders have an illustrious career ahead of them and will contribute to the country substantially.

It may be noted that in the last few years, the Northeast has witnessed many firsts that should actually have happened long, long ago. Almost 60 years after Nagaland attained statehood, the national anthem was played inside the Nagaland Assembly for the first time on 21 February 2021. Similarly, the Tripura Assembly played the national anthem for the first time on 23 March 2018 after the BJP government was sworn in the state. For the first time since our Independence, under PM Modi, our most far-flung villages on the border have been given top priority for development and employment generation under the recently launched Vibrant Village Programme. I can go on about the changes, but I would rather appeal to all Indians to travel to the Northeast and witness them first-hand.

I commend the authors of this book for meticulously documenting this historic journey. May this volume serve as a source of inspiration for all those who are committed to nation-building and sustainable progress. The story of Northeast India's transformation under PM Modi is not just a tale of development; it is a narrative of hope, empowerment and the unwavering belief in a brighter future for all.

—Jagat Prakash Nadda
National President, Bharatiya Janata Party

INTRODUCTION
Past Imperfect, Future Bright

Tuhin A. Sinha and Aditya Pittie

As Prime Minister (PM) Narendra Modi completed nine years in office in May 2023, several supporters, well-wishers and party workers listed what they felt were the biggest achievements of the National Democratic Alliance (NDA) government. Among the five most common and biggest achievements were:

a) Massive pan-India infrastructure overhaul[1]
b) India's economic resurgence to being the world's fifth largest economy in terms of gross domestic product (GDP)[2], a crucial contributor to it being the turnaround of PSU (public sector undertaking) banks from NPA (non-performing asset) hubs to profit reservoirs[3]
c) The huge digital revolution, best exemplified by the success

---

[1]'9 Years of Modi Govt: India Witnessed Fast-Paced Infrastructure Development in All Sectors in the Last Nine Years', *News Services Division All India Radio*, 25 May 2023, https://tinyurl.com/y38j392n. Accessed on 6 December 2023.

[2]PTI, 'India to Top Germany and Japan to Become Third Largest Economy by 2030: Survey', *India Today*, 25 October 2023, https://tinyurl.com/2fa89f2u. Accessed on 6 December 2023.

[3]Banerjee, Abhishek, and Karuna Gopal, 'The Great Turnaround : How Public Sector Banks Became Most Profitable in India', *Firstpost*, 17 August 2023, https://tinyurl.com/yer39wmt. Accessed on 6 December 2023.

of the unified payment interface (UPI) and CoWIN[4]

d) India's nuanced foreign policy[5] and defence sector overhaul[6]
e) Transformation of the Northeastern states of India

All of these and others are huge game changers, both from the point of view of manifesting our economic prowess in the years to come as well as securing our national interests.

While a lot has been said about the other aspects, the complete, all-pervasive transformation of our Northeastern states has often not received the attention that it deserves. Seamless connectivity, massive infrastructure development, peace, stability and inclusiveness have been the hallmarks of the transformation that these states have witnessed from 2014 onwards. In fact, the transformation that the region has witnessed in the last nine years makes one wonder what held it back for over seven decades. It intrigues us to think that a region as vast and crucial for the country was virtually abandoned by the Congress government at the time of the 1962 war. It hurts to think that connectivity to the region was never given the impetus it needed. As a result, many from the region still speak of a sense of abandonment since 1962. Until a decade ago, government servants working in the far-flung border districts of Arunachal Pradesh would sometimes take up to two days to reach the state capital, Itnanagar.

Was it, as some may call it, the 'tyranny of distance'? The ruling party's sheer inertia in moving beyond Lutyens' Delhi and

---

[4]Sharma, R.S., 'Digital Public Infrastructure: The Story of India's Digital Revolution', *The Indian Express*, 19 September 2023, https://tinyurl.com/4kc85xzc. Accessed on 6 December 2023.

[5]Chandra, Satish, 'Modi Government's Foreign Policy Has Been Transformative', 28 May 2023, *The Sunday Guardian*, https://tinyurl.com/9w4mdhzf, Accessed on 6 December 2023.

[6]Singh Nagial, Balwan, 'The Rising Story of the Indian Defence Industry from Importer to Exporter', *The Economic Times*, 1 April 2023, https://tinyurl.com/e2d4ves3. Accessed on 6 December 2023.

into the Northeastern hinterlands to comprehend what really ailed the region was appalling, to say the least. The stepmotherly treatment of the region was particularly disturbing, considering that these states were an integral part of the Indian nation from a cultural perspective as indicated by the ample evidence pointing to the region's inherent role in our ancient literature.

In the Mahabharata, Arjuna travelled the length and breadth of Bharat during his exile. When he came to ancient Manipur, he met Chitrangada, the daughter of the king of Manipur, and asked her father, Chitravahana, for her hand in marriage. The king stated that, according to the matrilineal customs of his people, the children born of Chitrangada were heirs to Manipur, and hence the princess could not be taken away from Manipur. Arjuna agreed to the stipulation that he would take away neither Chitrangada nor any children borne by her from Manipur and wed the princess on this premise. They begot a son, whom they named Babruvahana.

In the Kalika Purana, the famous Kamakhya Devi temple in Guwahati, which dates back 1,400 years, has been mentioned. The Kalika Purana describes Kamakhya as the yielder of all desires, the young bride of Shiva and the giver of salvation. The femininity and fertility of Shakti, the most powerful goddess in the Hindu pantheon, take the form of Kamakhya. The presence of Kamakhya denotes an extremely progressive inclusion in the Indian religious, cultural and knowledge systems—celebrated magnanimously in the region.

The cultural heritage of the Northeast is not the only link the region shares with the rest of India. It holds great significance from various perspectives. Before we come to decode the actual contours of the change that the Northeastern states have witnessed since 2014, let us briefly travel back two centuries in order to understand the larger picture.

A Brief History of the Region

Between 1817 and 1826, there were three Burmese invasions of Assam, leading to the control of Burma over the Ahom and Manipur kingdoms. Subsequently, the British engaged in the first Anglo-Burmese War against Burma, which ended with the British emerging victorious, thereby beginning the colonial period in the region.

Northeast India was first made a part of the Bengal Province in British India, which covered large parts of what is now South Asia and Southeast Asia. In the early twentieth century, the Northeastern states were established and became separated from their traditional trading partners, Bhutan and Myanmar. The city of Shillong had served as the capital of the Assam province and continued as the capital of undivided Assam until Meghalaya gained statehood in 1972. After Meghalaya's separation, the capital of Assam was shifted to Dispur, while Shillong became the capital of present-day Meghalaya.

The British influenced the conversion of certain communities in present-day Mizoram, Nagaland and Meghalaya to Christianity. As a result, the majority of the population in these regions today follows the Christian faith.

During World War II, Japan planned an invasion of India from Burma, leading to two significant battles—the Battle of Kohima and the Battle of Imphal. The Battle of Imphal took place from March to July 1944 in the vicinity of Imphal city. The Japanese forces suffered heavy losses and were defeated, forcing them to retreat to Burma. The Battle of Kohima occurred between 4 April and 22 June 1944, around the town of Kohima. It resulted in the defeat of the Japanese troops.

Following India's Independence from British rule in 1947, the Northeastern region of India comprised Assam and the princely states of Tripura and Manipur. The North-East Frontier Agency (NEFA), originally known as the North-East Frontier Tracts

(NEFT), was one of the political divisions in British India within the larger state of Assam and later the Republic of India until 20 January 1972, when it became the Union Territory of Arunachal Pradesh, along with some parts of Assam. Arunachal Pradesh subsequently became a state on 20 February 1987. On the same date, Mizoram which was earlier carved out of the Lushai Hills District of Assam in 1972 as a Union Territory (UT), also became a state.

Nagaland was established on 30 November 1963, followed by Meghalaya on 21 January 1972 and Mizoram in 1987, which were carved out of the larger territory of Assam. Manipur and Tripura remained Union Territories of India from 1956 until 1972, when they achieved full statehood. This group of seven states was commonly known as the 'Seven Sisters'. In 2002, Sikkim became the eighth state to be integrated into the North Eastern Council (NEC). The historic addition of Sikkim to Northeastern states was made by then PM Atal Bihari Vajpayee, who coined a new name for these states—Ashta Lakshmi (eight avatars of Goddess Lakshmi).

Right after Independence, the Northeastern region was plagued by multiple problems on various fronts. Southern Assam was caught in the storm of an unhindered mass migration of people from East Pakistan (now Bangladesh). Insecurity, uncertainty and chaos became an unalienable part of the lives of people living in the border districts. The first Chief Minister (CM) of Assam, Gopinath Bordoloi, wrote to the then Home Minister Sardar Vallabhbhai Patel in sheer exasperation: 'If Assam is to continue as part of India, it must be allowed to exercise the power of restricting the ingress of people not only for avoiding an economic breakdown but also maintaining communal harmony...'[7] The problem of illegal migration was to only grow by leaps and bounds in the decades to come, leading to a demographic distortion in many parts.

---

[7]Nag, Sajal, *Nehru and the North East*, Nehru Memorial Museum and Library, 2015.

In many isolated hilly districts of Arunachal Pradesh, Manipur and Nagaland, the resident tribals feared the invasion of outsiders, and hence the Inner Line Permit (ILP) had to be restored in large areas. Interestingly, apart from the cynicism towards outsiders, in almost every state there were conflicts, even among different Indigenous tribes. The central government in the initial decades neither had the understanding nor the interest to address these. This led to a prolonged alienation of these states that resulted in insurgent groups and violence taking centre stage for a very long time.

In 1962, tragedy struck with the Indo-China War, which most impartial commentators believe was the result of a horrible miscalculation by PM Jawaharlal Nehru. Prime Minister Nehru's apathetic address to the nation during the war caused a lot of anguish among the people of the region—a hurt Kiren Rijiju (Minister of Earth Sciences of India) has spoken of this rather candidly and mentioned in his essay, following in this book.

The unsavoury embarrassment of 1962 was followed by another dark chapter in March 1966. Prime Minister Indira Gandhi's government was caught unaware when the Mizo National Front (MNF), which was then an insurgent outfit, declared independence from India in the early hours of 1 March 1966. Following this declaration, MNF rebels launched coordinated attacks on the Indian army and paramilitary installations all over the Lushai Hills (the present-day state of Mizoram). Limited intelligence reports available with the central government pointed towards the collusion of East Pakistan, wherein the objective was for Lushai Hills to declare independence from India. Left with scant options, PM Indira Gandhi retaliated with brutality. On 5–6 March 1966, Indian Air Force (IAF) fighters rained incendiary bombs and strafed many urban clusters in the Lushai Hills District. As most people had already fled their homes to safer shelters, fearing violence, the death toll was limited. However, this unfortunate bombing of its own citizens due to prolonged mismanagement of the problem left an indelible scar in people's psyches and a trust deficit that only increased with time.

The late 1970s witnessed an unprecedented students' movement in Assam against the uncontrolled illegal migration from Bangladesh, which had now led to a large number of outsiders being settled across the state. This student movement was to later assume the form of a political movement and result in the formation of the Asom Gana Parishad (AGP) government in Assam in 1985, led by the then youngest CM in India, Prafulla Kumar Mahanta.

In all these decades, the natives and residents of Northeast India longed for a concrete change and a sense of belongingness that eluded them repeatedly. Despite the entire region being breathtakingly beautiful, tourist footfalls remained abysmally low. Insurgent attacks continued sporadically across the region and kept people from other parts of the country away. Interestingly, Delhi University (DU) had a good number of students enrolling every year from the Northeastern states. A one-way journey from their native place to Delhi would sometimes take them almost three days. The grit and determination of these students were admirable. Those were the days when people would get away with casual racist slurs aimed at these students, making their struggles in Delhi even tougher. Thankfully, the perversity has reduced enormously over the years, with the increased mainstreaming of these students and their regional pride.

In Modern Times

Our Northeastern region as it stands today, shares an international border of 5,182 km—about 99 per cent of its total geographical boundary—with several neighbouring countries. The region shares an international border of 1,395 km with China in the north, 1,640 km with Myanmar in the east, 1,596 km with Bangladesh in the southwest, 97 km with Nepal in the west and

455 km with Bhutan in the northwest. It comprises an area of 262,184 sq. km, almost 8 per cent of that of India. The Siliguri Corridor, a strip of land about 20 km wide, connects the region to the rest of mainland India. It boggles any sensible mind to think why such a vast landmass of crucial strategic significance was left under-attended or ignored for so many decades by so many successive Congress governments.

In September 2013, the United Progressive Alliance (UPA) government had told the Parliament that independent India had a policy for many years that the best defence was not to develop the border. An undeveloped border is safer than a developed border, the then defence minister said, adding that China had improved its infrastructure on the border.[8] Dr Manmohan Singh, who was a Rajya Sabha member from Assam during his term as PM, never once spoke on any issue specific to the Northeast.

With the cavalier, escapist attitude of earlier governments, the region continued to be a breeding ground for militancy for decades. There were around 600 Chinese border violations along the LAC (Line of Actual Control) between 2010 and 2013, with a majority of the violations being in the Northeast, against which, neither adequate action were taken, nor any attempt was made to improve the connectivity of the Northeast with other parts of the country. This cost the region significantly in terms of development.

What Changed Post 2014?

With the coming to power of the Bharatiya Janata Party (BJP) at the Centre, PM Narendra Modi saw immense potential for growth in the Northeastern states and embarked upon his ambitious Act East Policy. His positive intent for the Northeast is clear from his first tweet on the Northeast dated 29 November 2014 after

[8]PTI, 'Congress Leaders Should Recall Antony's Statement on Border Issue during UPA Rule: Kiren Rijiju', *The Times of India*, 12 October 2021, https://tinyurl.com/45mtus3e. Accessed on 21 September 2023.

becoming the PM. It says, 'Rich natural resources combined with talent of our youth gives our North-East the potential to play a key role in our development journey. India will not develop till the North-East develops.'[9]

He envisaged the Northeastern states as India's Gateway to Southeast Asia. To realize this potential, work is resolutely underway on projects like the India–Myanmar–Thailand Trilateral Highway (IMT Highway) and the Agartala–Akhaura rail project. Once complete, these would be complete game changers for the region.

When the outlook changes, the rest of the changes are mere formalities. Unlike most Indian PMs who did not challenge the status quo, PM Modi thrives on taking the uncharted route. Social justice and historical course correction are always high priorities, be it with regard to individuals or a region. As PM, he was clear right from the start that tapping the true potential of Northeastern states was to be the top priority for his government.

Major Developments under PM Modi

Seeing is believing: Unlike most PMs in the past who handled the Northeast from a distance, PM Modi has visited the Northeast around 60 times in nine years, which is perhaps more than the total number of visits by all his predecessors put together. The result is a miraculous transformation in the region, with the Northeast being cited all over as the Modi government's development model.

Act East Policy: In the last nine years, PM Modi has introduced a slew of measures and policies for the development of the Northeast. He saw immense potential for growth in the Northeastern states and embarked upon his Act East Policy. He envisaged the Northeastern states as India's trade gateway to Southeast Asia.

[9]'PM: We Are Committed to Realising the Potential of the North-East and Accelerating Its Progress', *pib.gov*, 29 November 2014, https://tinyurl.com/y3rd9mae. Accessed on 21 September 2023.

Increasing number of airports: Northeast India witnessed an unprecedented jump in the number of airports in the North Eastern Region (NER), which rose from nine to 16, and the numbers of flights have increased from about 900 to 1,900 post 2014. Some Northeastern states have made their way onto India's railway map for the first time and efforts are being made to expand the waterways too.

Connectivity: The major ongoing Capital Road Connectivity projects in NER include an alternate two-lane highway from Bagrakote to Pakyong (NH 717A) (152 km) in the Sikkim–Kalimpong–Darjeeling region, four-laning of Imphal–Moreh section of NH 39 (20 km), two-laning of 75.4 km in Manipur, four-laning of Dimapur–Kohima road (62.9 km) in Nagaland, four-laning of Nagaon bypass to Holongi (167 km) in Arunachal Pradesh and two-laning of Aizawl–Tuipang NH 54 (351 km) in Mizoram.

With Manipur being connected to our railway network in 2023, all Northeastern states now have access to basic rail connectivity. Now, the NER has embarked upon another ambitious plan to invest over ₹95,261 crore to execute 21 projects, including connecting the state capitals of Manipur, Mizoram and Meghalaya by 2023, and Nagaland by 2026.[10]

Decline in insurgency and removal of the Armed Forces (Special Powers) Act (AFSPA): In the past 9 years, Northeast India has witnessed a major dip in incidents of insurgency. According to the reports, there has been an 80 per cent dip in such incidences.[11] The central government has withdrawn the AFSPA from 60 per cent areas of Assam. In six districts of Manipur, AFSPA's operation

---

[10]'Railways to Invest over Rs 95,261 cr to Link Northeastern State Capitals', *Business Standard*, 4 June 2022, https://tinyurl.com/mr67jzbk. Accessed on 21 September 2023.

[11]Chauhan, Neeraj, 'Insurgency-Related Incidents Dipped by 80% In N-E States Last Year: MHA Data', *Hindustan Times*, 2 March 2021, https://tinyurl.com/2xjzut25. Accessed on 6 December 2023.

is limited to 15 police stations. In Arunachal Pradesh, only one district remains covered under AFSPA. In Nagaland, AFSPA has been lifted from seven districts, and in Tripura and Meghalaya, it has been completely lifted.

5G connectivity: Prime Minister Modi's government is working relentlessly on improving digital connectivity in the Northeast by enhancing the optical fibre network. 5G will play a pivotal role in the development of the start-up ecosystem and the service sector, among others in the region.

Impetus to natural farming: Prime Minister Modi's government has also earmarked a pivotal development for the Northeast when it comes to natural farming. Through the Krishi UDAN scheme, the farmers in the region are able to send their products across the country and the world. In fact, in the last 6 years, the region has reported 85 per cent growth in the export of agricultural products.[12] It goes without saying that the improved infrastructure and communications have played a crucial role in this change.

Rising political stature and representation: Northeast India today, has the highest-ever representation in the Union Council of Ministers wherein there are two cabinet ministers and three ministers of state. For the first time, a Member of Parliament (MP) from Tripura has found a place in the Council of Ministers.

Cultural outreach: Over the years, Nagaland's biggest annual cultural extravaganza, the Hornbill Festival and Manipur's Sangai Festival have been attracting visitors from all parts of the country. Prime Minister Modi inaugurated the Hornbill Festival in 2014, within months of becoming the PM. He has spoken about the Northeastern states several times on his radio show and encouraged people to visit these states. He has invoked the

---

[12]Anand, Saurav, 'Northeast India Sees over 85% Agricultural Product Export Growth in Last 6 Years', *Livemint*, 2 December 2022, https://tinyurl.com/3rwvakzn. Accessed on 21 September 2023.

legacy and contribution of Lachit Borphukan and Rani Gaidinliu to our nation, making the country aware of these icons. All of these gestures have instilled a new confidence in the natives of Northeast India. Today, people from the Northeast travel across the country and settle in other parts of the country with a new confidence, knowing fully well that the PM of the nation is constantly rooting for them.

Beyond Data and Statistics

While the data indicates the level of change in the Northeast, for an inquisitive writer and assimilator of information, it sparks our curiosity to decode this transformation and democratize it as much as possible. How does one do that? By letting the real facilitators, executors, researchers and witnesses of this change talk about this journey. This is also what makes this book very special.

So, for the first time, Himanta Biswa Sarma, the dynamic CM of Assam, writes about his war against drugs and its significance for the entire region. In another first, Pema Khandu, CM of Arunachal Pradesh, writes about how he zealously ensured that the backward-most districts of Arunachal Pradesh were among the first to catch up on digital governance. Kiren Rijiju, Central Minister for Earth Sciences, writes about the path-breaking Vibrant Village Programme that accords first priority to the development of villages on the border. Baijayant Panda, a former MP and BJP incharge for Assam, gives an overview of the cultural as well as infrastructural changes that have been at the core of the Northeast's recent transformation. The BJP's youth wing, Bharatiya Janta Yuva Morcha (BJYM) Chief Tejasvi Surya writes about how PM Modi's policies have leveraged a new energy in the youth of the region.

Alexander Laloo Hek, minister for animal husbandry, Meghalaya government, writes about his tenure as health minister of Meghalaya when PM Modi led the nation's fight against the

Covid-19 pandemic. Anthropologist Rami N. Desai decodes the ethnic clashes in the region and how the government has made diligent efforts to minimize them. Dr Ankita Dutta explains Himanta Biswa's relentless efforts to save Assam from 'outsiders'. Rajya Sabha MP Phagnon Konyak and Tage Rita, an agricultural entrepreneur from Arunachal, bring forth the women's perspective of belonging to the region, witnessing its transformation and contributing to the change. Member of Parliament Raju Bista, policy expert Vaibhav Dange, and journalist Karma Paljor decode the infrastructure turnaround in detail. Author and policy expert Aashish Chandorkar writes about the changes in the health sector in the Northeast, whereas psephologist Pradeep Bhandari decodes the change in voting patterns and the impact of PM Modi.

It would be unfair if we didn't mention Manipur here. When we started working on the book, Manipur, like the other Northeastern states, was surging ahead with its developmental targets. Unfortunately, starting the first week of May 2023, the entire developmental narrative took a backseat as large-scale violence broke out in the state. Unfortunately, Manipur saw a prolonged spell of ethnic violence after many years. While the worst is behind us now, we felt it was appropriate to include a chapter that talks about the positive transformation that the state has witnessed in the last few years. While the government stands committed to eradicating violence, and the recent tripartite peace agreement signed between the Centre and the Manipur government with Manipur's oldest insurgent outfit, the United National Liberation Front (UNLF) on 30 November 2023 bears testimony to this, not talking about the governance transformation in Manipur since 2014, would have been unfair to the state. As we write this, our hearts go out to the people of Manipur, who have suffered loss and suffering.

As this book endeavours to capture the remarkable journey of the Northeast, it's crucial to acknowledge that some of the data used in the chapters is sourced from classified official records as the authors were directly involved in the execution of the concerned schemes. There could be a mild disparity between this data and that which is available on public domain.

A book is always a humble start. In the years and decades to come, if powered by PM Modi's transformational push, the region is able to emerge as an economic powerhouse for the world while retaining the best principles of environment conservation and sustainable living; if it can become a hub of free trade between India and the entire Eastern world while retaining its distinctively plural cultural identity; this book would take pride in having been the first of its kind in showcasing the Northeast to the world.

1

A NEW ASSAM

Himanta Biswa Sarma

लोकरञ्जनमेवात्र राज्ञां धर्मः सनातनः
सत्यस्य रक्षणं चैव व्यवहारस्य चार्जवम।।

It is the foremost duty of a ruler to keep his subjects happy and gain their confidence. In the same manner, it is also his duty to always uphold the truth and maintain honesty and sincerity in his behaviour.

In the Shanti Parva of the Mahabharata, Bhishma Pitamah gives the aforementioned treatise on Rajdharma—or the principles of governance—to Dharmaraj Yudhishthira. This ancient wisdom of Rajdharma serves as an inspiration to public servants like me. When I became the Chief Minister (CM) of Assam on 10 May 2021, I sought to emulate these ideals. In front of me was the inspirational story of Prime Minister (PM) Narendra Modi, a man who has always lived up to the ideals of Rajdharma and served as an embodiment of righteousness. In 2014, he undertook a series of mammoth confidence-building initiatives to gain the trust of the people of the Northeast and win over their hearts with sincere love and devotion.

As a result, when I took office, my mission was clear—I had to take forward the vision of PM Modi and implement his policies on the ground. We have envisioned an Assam where we eliminate the problems faced by the people of Assam and script a new destiny for their future. Upon assuming office, we undertook various administrative reforms to improve governance. For example, we took the decision to hold weekly Cabinet meetings so as to make sure we are regularly communicating and updating ourselves to best govern the people of Assam. We have also held Cabinet meetings outside the capital, decentralizing governance quite literally and taking it to different districts and towns. Through such measures, we have been able to take decisions and implement policies that have laid the foundation of a new Assam. Our double-engine government has been working in the relentless pursuit of Rajdharma through various avenues, as detailed below.

Economic Emergence

The first major challenge we faced after assuming office was to improve the economic growth of a state that has historically been plagued by insurgency and militancy. Assam was lagging behind in key aspects of health, education and infrastructure. The state had minimal business activity, despite its tremendous potential. The first step towards regenerating economic growth was the construction of infrastructure and then the clearing up of legal and administrative bottlenecks. This was a process that had speedily begun since 2014.

Assam in particular has witnessed unprecedented development in recent times, with the addition of several newly constructed bridges, the expansion of roads and highways and the ongoing construction of a tunnel under the Brahmaputra. This infrastructural boost gives massive headroom for connectivity via road, air and sea, fostering economic growth.

These measures by the Union government are being complemented in Assam by our state government policies that promote ease of doing business. With the decriminalization of labour laws[1], we have eliminated the risk of imprisonment for economic offences that do not involve mala fide. We have also repealed 364 old Acts to reduce the compliance burden on citizens and businesses.[2] With a cheap land bank made available for industrial use, Assam paved the way for investors to establish manufacturing and other industries in the state. The state currently boasts over 50 industrial parks with sector-specific infrastructure, an industrial zone of 99.4 miles along the National Highways near Guwahati and the only industrial growth centre in India with access to four countries within 750 km at Matia. The latter is the most crucial, as India's total exports to Bangladesh, Myanmar, Bhutan and Nepal stand at $17 billion, making Assam India's gateway to the Association of Southeast Asian Nations (ASEAN) and the Asia-Pacific.[3]

If we purely look at numbers, Assam's gross domestic product (GDP) and per capita income have grown at unprecedented rates since 2014. The steep rise is a proof of the central government's constant push for the development of Assam and the Northeast. The result of these measures has been that the gross state domestic product (GSDP) of Assam for 2023–24 (at current prices) is projected to be ₹5.67 lakh crore, amounting to growth of 15 per cent over 2022–23. In 2022–23, Assam's per capita income (at current prices) was estimated to be ₹118,504, an increase of 15 per cent over 2021–22. In 2022–23, India's per capita income was estimated to increase by 14 per cent to ₹170,620.[4] According to the Periodic Labour Force Survey, in 2021–22, Assam's unemployment

---

[1]Kalita, Prabin, 'Assam Govt Proposes to Remove Jail Provision for Violation of Labour Laws', *The Times of India,* 21 December 2022, http://tinyurl.com/2p8c2kcc. Accessed on 5 September 2023.

[2]For this and other instances where specific sources have not been provided for the figures, these are drawn from files privy to the Chief Minister's office.

[3]Borooah, Nabaarun, 'Paradigm Shift in Assam's Outlook Towards Business', *The Sentinel*, 23 February 2023, https://tinyurl.com/5n8ca3cx. Accessed on 24 September 2023.

[4]'Assam Budget Analysis 2023-24', *PRS Legislative Research,* https://tinyurl.com/3nctvk6x. Accessed on 24 September 2023.

rate was 4.9 per cent (as per current weekly status), lower than the national unemployment rate of 6.6 per cent.

Currently, we are also working to calculate the GDP at the district level so as to understand the economic conditions of each district and work towards achieving equitable economic progress throughout the state. These various steps taken by the state government, coupled with the Centre's push for strengthening geographical connectivity through building robust road and railway infrastructure along with building new airports, gave Assam the title of 'Most improved big state' by *India Today*.[5]

A Model of Women-Centric Development

The empowerment of women is essential for the holistic growth and social development of families, which in turn benefit communities. When women are included in the economic planning of a country, the workforce is strengthened with exclusive skill sets. Furthermore, women who are educated and conscious of their choices, potential and importance can live dignified and productive lives. This leads to diverse talents at workplaces, happier families and healthier children.

This rapid scale of economic growth and development has not come at the cost of economic inequality as is often the case. In fact, we have taken a holistic approach to bring in interconnected development in terms of both economic outcomes and social upliftment. Policy decisions for the upliftment of women, especially from various marginalized communities, have attained great success.

For example, our flagship schemes, such as Orunodoi and microfinance loan waiver, have been targeted towards empowering women, especially those belonging to low-income families. Today,

[5]Deka, Kaushik, 'Most Improved Big State: Assam | Ahead of the Curve', *India Today*, 26 December 2022, http://tinyurl.com/3bbwjzw5. Accessed on 5 September 2023.

Orunodoi provides ₹1,250 every month to women from 27 lakh households directly in their bank accounts to help them meet daily necessities such as food, medicine and electricity.[6] Currently, we are also working out a plan to increase the Orunodoi monthly sum from ₹1,250 to ₹1,400.

Moreover, to provide relief to women borrowers of microfinance, especially the debt-ridden women borrowers whose bank accounts have become non-performing assets, we have launched the Assam Micro Finance Incentive and Relief Scheme (AMFIRS). Under categories I and II of the scheme, around 10 lakh female borrowers have been provided assistance worth approximately ₹1,780 crore.[7] We have also supported many women's self-help groups to organize and empower themselves through the production of indigenous handloom and handicraft products, creating an independent women-centric village economy.

Giant Leaps in Healthcare and Education

Improving the healthcare and education sectors of the state has been one of our primary goals. The All India Institute of Medical Sciences (AIIMS) Guwahati[8] was inaugurated and dedicated to the nation by PM Narendra Modi on 14 April 2023, along with three new medical colleges at Kokrajhar, Nalbari and Nagaon. In addition, nine medical colleges are being built at Lakhimpur, Dhubri, Nalbari, Tinsukia, Nagaon, Kokrajhar, Charaideo and Biswanath.

We have also upgraded the existing schools in the state. Tele-education infrastructure has been set up in 1,859 schools

[6]'Assam Orunodoi Scheme 2023: Application Form, Orunodoi Beneficiary List', *Pm Modi Yojana*, 13 November 2023, http://tinyurl.com/h9hxwdzh. Accessed on 5 September 2023.

[7]For this and other figures for which no separate source has been provided, the information has been drawn from sources privy to the chief minister's office.

[8]The hospital has 750 beds (including 30 for AYUSH).

(1,319 upper primary and 540 secondary schools) and five studios have been established for remote teaching using e-content from broadcasting[9]—two in Guwahati and one each in Kokrajhar, Diphu and Dhemaji. An additional 350 tele-classrooms—classrooms where classes can be taught via a conference call—are to be established in August 2023 in 350 secondary schools under State Owned Priority Development (SOPD). Smart classrooms, which allow the integration of audiovisual and multimedia modes of teaching into the curriculum, have also been implemented in 4,070 upper primary and secondary schools. As many as 51,789 tablet PCs have been provided to 44,536 schools (all government/provincialized elementary, secondary and senior secondary schools) for accessing the Shiksha Setu portal and monitoring apps and for encouraging e-learning for students and school management, thereby digitizing education for the twenty-first century.

Employment and Entrepreneurship

When we first took office in May 2021, Assam faced the problem of rampant unemployment. We endeavoured to give one lakh government jobs to our able youth while also giving incentives for entrepreneurs and start-ups to transform job seekers into job givers. We have recruited 41,920 capable people for various government posts since May 2021. On 25 May 2023, we recruited 45,401 people to Grade III and IV posts after conducting transparent examinations. This mammoth job recruitment drive has taken us closer to realizing the vision of one lakh government jobs.

Additionally, we have launched the Swami Vivekananda Assam Youth Empowerment (SVAYEM) Scheme and other programmes to provide skill-training to the youth and fund budding entrepreneurs. For example, under the renewed SVAYEM

---

[9]'ICT in Education', *Government of Assam Elementary Education Samagra Siksha Assam*, https://tinyurl.com/35e3389u. Accessed on 6 December 2023.

scheme, we will provide ₹50,000 to two lakh youth so that they can build their start-ups and help provide employment to others.

An interesting story for us has been the settlement of the closure of Hindustan Paper Corporation Limited (HPCL) paper mills. The closing of the two mills had become a boiling issue in the state, as employees had lost their jobs when the two public sector undertakings (PSUs) closed without notice, becoming non-performing assets. We saw an opportunity in this event. Our government took part in the auction of the assets, bought the land, cleared the debt and offered a rehabilitation package to mill employees. We have also re-employed qualified candidates during our job drive. This is the first time a state government has stepped in and saved people from a time of crisis that was created by a private enterprise.

Heralding a New Era of Peace

To bring peace and prosperity to the state, we have initiated several welfare measures for men and women in uniform and their families. We spend more than many states in India on police reform and welfare. For better housing facilities and improving the quality of life of police personnel and their families, a project has been taken up for redevelopment of the Police Reserve at Guwahati for ₹544.54 crore.[10]

For several decades, the Northeast has been torn with border conflicts, militancy and other issues. Starting from 2021, the governments of Assam, Meghalaya, Arunachal Pradesh, Mizoram and Nagaland adopted a unique policy to resolve border disputes, aided by Union Home Minister Amit Shah. All states formed five-member regional committees headed by a state Cabinet minister and included bureaucrats and local representatives. These bodies visited each and every disputed area, analysed the exchange of

[10]Government of Assam, *A Year of Good Governance*, 5 July 2022, https://tinyurl.com/bdyynjx3. Accessed on 24 September 2023.

land records, conducted detailed deliberations and negotiations, and sent the final recommendations to their respective state governments, upon which various CM-level and Cabinet-level talks and negotiations were held to clearly demarcate the disputed sites so as to reflect the will of the people.

As a result, on 29 March and 20 April 2023, we announced the resolution of long-standing border disputes between Assam and both Meghalaya and Arunachal Pradesh in the presence of Union Home Minister Amit Shah. These are extremely significant developments that have paved the way for ensuring long-lasting peace in the Northeastern region.

There have been significant efforts to bring long-lasting peace by holding talks with militant outfits and rehabilitating surrendered militants by offering financial packages. We have signed various accords with student unions and militant groups for peace in the region, the most recent ones being the Karbi Peace Accord, Assam Adivasi Peace Accord, Dimasa Peace Accord and Bodo Peace Accord, which brought an end to the Bodoland secessionist movement. Additionally, lucrative rehabilitation packages have been provided to surrendered militants to further encourage others to follow the path towards peace. These developments have further led to the repeal of the Armed Forces (Special Powers) Act (AFSPA) from the state, heralding a new era of peace.

War on Drugs

When we assumed office, we had to shoulder the enormous task of eradicating the illegal international drug trade, which by this point had become a well-established network. In order to combat drug traffickers, we granted the Assam Police operational freedom to break the supply chain from the entry point to the peddlers, leaving them without supplies and eventually guaranteeing that it does not reach the general populace. A citizen-centric strategy was chosen, focusing on raising awareness to turn individuals into active members of the anti-drug movement. According to statistics from the Crime Investigation Department (CID), Assam Police, the total number of crimes that are now being reported has increased by almost nine times, while the number of arrests has increased by almost seven times between 2018 and 2022.

Since the new state government took over in May 2021, a total of 5,110 cases have been registered, 8,484 people have been arrested and 734 vehicles have been seized under the Narcotic Drugs and Psychotropic Substances Act, 1985. Additionally, 689 *bigha* of cannabis and opium cultivation have also been destroyed. As of 20 February 2023, successive police operations have recovered drugs and cash worth ₹1,274.63 crore.

Our 'war on drugs' has proved to be an effective strategy to counter drug trafficking in India. By adopting a multi-pronged approach that involves enforcement measures and public awareness campaigns, we have been able to disrupt the supply chain of drugs, arrest traffickers and reduce the demand for drugs. The seizure of large quantities of drugs and the arrest of several notorious dealers is a testament to the success of the government's efforts.

Crackdown on Child Marriage

Assam has long trailed behind in crucial healthcare metrics like birth and death rates, which also contribute to the state's low human development index (HDI) ranking. For the years 2018–20, the state's maternal mortality rate was 195 deaths per one lakh live births. Compared to the present national rate of 97 deaths per one lakh live births, the previous rate was much higher. With 36 deaths per 1,000 live births in the year 2020, Assam would likewise have the highest infant mortality rate in the Northeast. Compared to the national average of 28 fatalities per 1,000 live births, this was disturbingly higher. This prompted us to announce a state-wide crackdown on child marriage because it leads to premature pregnancies, causing health hazards to both mother and child.

Over 2,000 people were detained within a day of the government's decision to crack down on child marriage. Of the 4,200 plus cases that have been reported, 3,500 have been reported by citizens, making it truly a people's movement. Of the more 6,800 plus defendants who have been named, 3,200 have already been taken into custody. It demonstrates that our strong-handed approach has been effective in both locating and apprehending offenders.

My Cabinet issued an order designating the secretary of each panchayat as a Child Marriage Prohibition Officer, giving the officer the authority to report child marriages that take place in the officer's village to the police. Bal panchayats and village-level gatherings, have been started in Cachar to educate locals about the negative impacts of child marriage.

Securing the Rights of Indigenous People

The immigration problem is a long-drawn-out saga that began before India attained independence. In the late 1930s and early 1940s, Syed Muhammed Saadulah, the premier of the state who helmed the Muslim League government, undertook an extensive land settlement policy called the Line System as a part of his 'Grow More Food' campaign, where lakhs of Bengali-speaking Muslim migrants from erstwhile East Bengal were settled as agricultural labourers in the districts of Lower Assam, particularly Barpeta, Goalpara and Barak Valley.

In 1971, the Indo-Pakistan War triggered a humanitarian crisis that led to over 10 million Bangladeshis settling in refugee camps in Tripura, Meghalaya, West Bengal and particularly Assam. In 1979, draft enrolments in Mangaldoi bypolls showed 47,000 doubtful entries, out of which 26,000 were confirmed to be outsiders. The inclusion of several foreigners in the electoral roll led to indigenous Assamese people from all walks of life coming together for a massive agitation against the demographic invasion of the state, demanding revised electoral rolls in the entire state. The Assam Andolan intensified and continued for two more years until the signing of the Assam Accord in 1985. However, the problem was far from over and the Accord provided little to no solution for the demographic invasion of Assam.

After repeated attempts, the Election Commission of India published a final delimitation order for the Assembly and Parliamentary constituencies, which gives newfound hope to the people of Assam.[11] Many new seats have been created to accommodate indigenous populations in Upper Assam, such as Makum, Sissiborgaon, Demow, Ranganadi, etc. At the same time, the number of constituencies has also increased for reserved areas of hill tribes such as Karbis, Bodos and Dimasas. For instance, Karbi Anglong now has six Scheduled Tribes (ST) seats instead of five. The delimitation exercise solves the most long-standing issue that has been the central theme of Assamese politics. It seeks to achieve the important task of ensuring that the indigenous people of Assam have the final say in determining the destiny of Assam's politics.

Additionally, we have taken steps to free up encroached lands, especially those surrounding the most sacred Barpeta and Batadraba[12] (Nangaon district) *Satra*s. These actions have gone a long way in restoring the glory of our magnificent satras and centres of Assamese Ekasarana Dharma. We are also working towards transforming the Nilachal Hills into a Maa Kamakhya Devi Corridor on the lines of Kashi and Ujjain, which will not only promote pilgrimage and tourism but also enhance the civilizational glory and prowess of Assamese socio-cultural life.

---

[11]'ECI Publishes Final Delimitation Order for Assembly & Parliamentary Constituencies of State of Assam, after Extensive Consultations with Stakeholders', *pib.gov*, 11 August 2023, https://tinyurl.com/3yasx833. Accessed on 24 September 2023.

[12]'Land around Assam Monastery to Be Reserved for Indigenous People', *The Hindu*, 24 September 2023, https://tinyurl.com/5c23rbj2. Accessed on 6 December 2023.

Asserting Assamese Culture

On 13 April 2023, a historical moment unfolded as over 11,304 Bihu dancers, artists and instrumentalists etched their names in golden letters, setting the record for the largest Bihu dance performance at a single venue in the Guinness Book of World Records' folk dance category.[13] This momentous achievement was a source of great pride for the state of Assam.

The people of Assam celebrated the 400th birth anniversary of her bravest son, Bir Lachit Borphukan, with great splendour. On that occasion too, the state made it to the Guinness Book of World Records in the 'Largest Online Photo Album of Handwritten Notes' section with the entry of over 42.94 lakh handwritten essays on the folk hero.[14]

The commemoration of the 400th birth anniversary of Lachit Borphukan was a grand and impressive event, spanning three days, held in the national capital. Dignitaries such as PM Narendra Modi, Home Minister Amit Shah, and other notable Union Ministers graced the occasion with their presence. In the lead-up to this event, the streets, bridges and even the metro trains of Delhi were adorned with the image of the Ahom general. This was not simply a celebration of an Assamese hero but a tribute to a national icon, an honour seldom witnessed before.

In December 2022, the Centre bestowed the long-awaited geographical indication (GI) tag on the *gamosa*, marking a momentous occasion for Assam's most revered article. The significance of this recognition cannot be overstated, as it affirms the unique cultural identity of the state. Notably, the gamosa has also gained popularity beyond Assam's borders, with influential

---

[13]'"Bihu" Performance with 11,304 Dancers, Drummers Enters Guinness World Records', *The Economic Times*, 13 April 2023, https://tinyurl.com/yey38xes. Accessed on 6 September 2023.

[14]'Largest Online Photo Album of Handwritten Notes', *The Guinness Book of World Records*, http://tinyurl.com/s7uhw3ym. Accessed on 5 September 2023.

personalities such as PM Modi adorning it—be it during his various tours throughout the country or his Yoga Day programme in New York City. This has helped to propel the gamosa onto the world stage, further enhancing its significance and recognition.

Externally Aided Projects

Assam has also been blessed by several externally aided projects supported by various central government agencies under the guidance of Finance Minister Nirmala Sitharaman.

The state government has laid special emphasis on the implementation of the central government's flagship programmes. Schemes like Jal Jeevan Mission (JJM), Pradhan Mantri Awas Yojana (PMAY), Pradhan Mantri Jan Arogya Yojana (PMJAY), etc., have been implemented successfully across the state. Steps have also been taken to ensure that the scheme benefits reach more and more targeted beneficiaries in a hassle-free manner.

The 120 MW Lower Kopili Hydro Electric Project funded by the Asian Development Bank, is expected to be completed by December 2024. Further, a memorandum of understanding (MoU) for setting up a 24 MW Karbi Langpi Middle-II Hydro Power Project for ₹300.70 crore in West Karbi Anglong has been signed between the Assam Power Generation Corporation Limited (APGCL) and Karbi Anglong Autonomous Council. We are also working towards generating 3,000 MW of solar power in the state by 2026. As part of this, three solar power projects have been inaugurated in Amguri, Udalguri, Samaguri, Cachar and Boko over the past 24 months. The government has approved a joint venture (JV) agreement between APGCL and Oil India Limited (OIL) for setting up 25 MW solar plant at Namrup in August last year.

A Bright Future

The transformation of Assam under the BJP-led government, with the unwavering support of PM Modi, has been nothing short of remarkable. Together, we have ushered in an era of progress, development and prosperity for the people of Assam. Through our comprehensive and inclusive approach, we have focussed on key sectors such as infrastructure, education, healthcare, agriculture and tourism, aiming to uplift every citizen and ensure a better quality of life. Our initiatives, including Orunodoi, SVAYEM, and the construction of roads, railways, bridges, hospitals and schools, have touched the lives of millions, providing them with accessible healthcare, improved connectivity and avenues for skill development and entrepreneurship.

We have taken significant steps to address long-standing issues such as illegal immigration and insurgency, fostering a sense of security and stability in the state. Our commitment to eliminating social menaces such as drugs and child marriage has played a crucial role in safeguarding peace and security, while other measures such as delimitation, freeing Satra lands, celebration of Bihu, etc., seeks to promote the indigenous people of Assam.

Furthermore, the focus on sustainable development and environmental conservation has ensured that Assam's rich biodiversity and natural resources are protected for future generations. Initiatives like the Guwahati Clean and Green campaign and the Kaziranga Anti-Poaching Task Force (including the Rhino Task Force) demonstrate our commitment to preserving the state's ecological treasures. For example, for the first time in history, not a single rhino was killed in Kaziranga in a whole calendar year in 2022.

The tireless efforts of PM Modi and his unwavering support for Assam have been instrumental in our journey towards transformation. His visionary policies and schemes, such as the Act East Policy and the Atmanirbhar Bharat Abhiyan, have provided us with the necessary framework to leverage our strengths and accelerate our development.

As we move forward, there is still much work to be done. We must continue to focus on bridging the urban-rural divide, empowering our youth and creating more employment opportunities. We must strive to enhance our education system, promote innovation and harness the potential of digital technologies to create a knowledge-based society.

I am confident that with the continued support of PM Modi and the collective efforts of the people of Assam, we will overcome any challenges that lie ahead and achieve greater heights of progress. Together, we will build a vibrant, inclusive, and prosperous Assam where every individual can fulfil their aspirations and contribute to the nation's growth.

Jai Hind! Joi Aai Axom!

2

EMPOWERING BORDER VILLAGES FOR GROWTH AND DEVELOPMENT

Kiren Rijiju

The North Eastern Region (NER) of India had long suffered due to its physical distance from New Delhi and an unbridgeable emotional gap from the central government. There are several factors responsible for it. One of the main reasons was that, for decades after the Independence of India, no central government made a genuine attempt to reach out and understand the issues of the people of the Northeast. The region itself is very diverse with several different tribes, cultural practices and conflicts. The negligence created severe isolation in people's minds.

On 20 January 1972 Arunachal Pradesh was carved out as a Union Territory (UT) for better administrative focus. On 20 February 1987, it became a full-fledged state. However, real change eluded the state as there was no genuine political outreach. Our former Prime Minister (PM) Shri Atal Bihari Vajpayee was the first PM to show real intent for development of the NER. He conceived a separate ministry for this purpose and initially set up a department for the development of NER. Sikkim was included as a member of the North Eastern Council (NEC) and mobile phone connectivity was launched in the region for the first time. Furthermore, the Pradhan Mantri Gram Sadak Yojana (PMGSY) was significantly expanded to benefit the NER.

I became a Member of Parliament (MP) in 2004 and started raising important issues related to the Northeast in Parliament. However, the United Progressive Alliance (UPA) government was lethargic. Prime Minister Manmohan Singh would only sparingly visit the region despite being a Rajya Sabha MP from Assam. Development projects, therefore, remained slow and was nowhere near the scale that was required for the region.

After Vajpayee ji's efforts between 1998–2004, a real change in the central government's attitude towards the Northeast finally became visible in 2014. Under the visionary leadership of PM Narendra Modi, a remarkable transformation has taken place in the last nine years. The Modi government's commitment to the Northeast has been nothing short of extraordinary. With the implementation of the Act East Policy, the Modi government has worked tirelessly to bridge the emotional gap and address the long-standing neglect of the Northeast. The Act East Policy has not only focussed on filling the infrastructure deficit in the region but has also made it a reservoir for growth and development. The people of the Northeast have experienced a newfound sense of ownership, which had been absent for decades.

If I start talking about all the development projects undertaken by the Modi government in the last nine years, it might take me over nine hours to elaborate. Therefore, let me focus on the most recent, yet the most transformative initiative—the Vibrant Village Programme, which aims to revolutionize our outlook towards border villages, making them the first priority and pillars of growth in their respective states.

The Vibrant Village Programme

The Vibrant Village Programme (VVP) is a visionary initiative launched by the Modi government to empower and uplift our border villages. It recognizes that these villages, which have so far been overlooked and marginalized, have immense potential for growth and development. The programme aims to make them the primary focus of attention and foster their socio-economic progress.

These border villages which are the most vulnerable in a hostile atmosphere of conflict, long deserved the best facilities. The fact that these villages were consistently ignored by successive governments over several decades, amounted to grave injustice which has finally been corrected by PM Modi.

Under the leadership of PM Narendra Modi, the Government of India (GoI) has approved the VVP with central components of ₹4,800 crore including ₹2,500 crore exclusively for road connectivity for the Financial Year (FY) 2022–23 to 2025–26. The VVP is a centrally sponsored scheme under which 2,967 villages in 46 blocks of 19 districts abutting northern border in the states of Arunachal Pradesh, Sikkim, Uttarakhand, Himachal Pradesh and the UT of Ladakh have been identified for comprehensive development. In the first phase, 662 villages have been identified with priority on coverage, which includes 455 villages in Arunachal Pradesh.

The VVP will help in improving the quality of life of the people living in identified border villages and encourage people to stay in their native locations, thereby reversing the outmigration from these villages and adding to the security of the border. District administration, with the help of appropriate mechanisms at block and panchayat level, will prepare action plans for identified villages to ensure 100 per cent saturation of central and state schemes. The focus areas of interventions identified for development of villages include road connectivity, drinking water, electricity, solar and wind energy, mobile and internet connectivity, tourist centres, multipurpose centres, healthcare infrastructure and wellness centres.

Through this programme, the government will help make the border villages with sparse population with limited connectivity and infrastructure, become self-sufficient. Under this scheme, the border villages will be provided with infrastructure, housing, tourist centres, road connectivity, provisioning of decentralized renewable energy, direct-to-home access for Doordarshan and educational channels, and support for livelihood generation. For best execution of the VVP, action plans for identified villages would be prepared by the district administration with assistance from the proper mechanisms at the block and panchayat levels, in order to guarantee complete saturation of federal and state programmes.

In the first week of March 2023, I had visited Monigong, an extremely tough village on the Indo-China border to review ground-level work undertaken thus far by the local administrator under this programme. Monigong is nearly 500 km from Itanagar and extremely far-flung. However, I could sense a new energy in local officials and new hope among the people. The local population in these villages never had any interaction with top leaders. However, now when we visit them, they realize that we are seriously working towards improving their lives. This reassurance is very important for the people living in a border village.

The Union Home Minister and Minister of Cooperation Shri Amit Shah, launched the VVP at Kibithoo—our easternmost border village in Arunachal Pradesh, on 10 April 2023. On the same day, Shri Amit Shah also inaugurated nine micro hydel projects of Arunachal government and 14 infrastructure projects worth ₹120 crore, which complement the overall border development plans for Arunachal Pradesh.

The impact of the VVP can already be witnessed in various border villages across the Northeast. Improved infrastructure has enhanced accessibility, leading to increased economic activities and investments. Employment opportunities have been created, reducing migration from the region. Social welfare initiatives have improved healthcare services, education and women's empowerment. The programme has also helped preserve and promote the unique cultural heritage of the Northeast, fostering a sense of pride and identity among the local communities.

The VVP stands as a testament to the Modi government's commitment to the overall development of the Northeast region. By recognizing the untapped potential of border villages and addressing their specific needs, the programme has taken flight to bridge the emotional gap that has persisted for decades. The transformative impact of the programme is already visible, and with continued focus and dedication, it is waiting to record a lasting positive change in the lives of those living in the border villages of the Northeast.

Unlike the previous governments, the Modi government has impeccable credentials of walking the talk on what it promises. Barely 10 days after Shri Amit Shah's visit to Kibithoo village, the GoI announced the completion of installation of 254 new 4G network towers and made them operational in 336 villages.

The move will provide the much-needed Internet and broadband connectivity to at least 70,000 residents in the villages near the Line of Actual Control (LAC) in the Indian territory. Under the 4G saturation project, out of 2,424 sites for 4G services in the Northeast, 270 sites will be connected through optical fibre, 1,237 through microwave and 917 sites will be connected through very small aperture terminal (VSAT).

Telecom and Internet connectivity makes a huge difference to some of these far-flung villages. For the Kibithoo Village in lower Dibang Valley, this is the first time they are experiencing direct communication facilities with the rest of the world. Similarly, for the Zemithang Village in Tawang, which bore the brunt of Chinese incursions in 1962, this seamless connectivity with the rest of the country marks an incredible change in their lives. It goes without saying that the 4G services in our border villages will hugely benefit our border security forces and improve our security apparatus.

I will end by quoting what Home Minister Amit Shah had asserted at the Kibithoo village. 'The era is gone when anyone could encroach on our lands. Now, not even land equal to '*sui ki noke*' (needlepoint) can be encroached,' he had roared while addressing the gathering at Kibithoo. I wish an Indian leader had shown the same ownership towards the people of Arunachal [then NEFA (North-East Frontier Agency)] way back in 1962. Had it been so, Arunachal would have been a different story.

I wish to thank PM Narendra Modi for the important representation he has provided to the elected MPs from the Northeast in his Cabinet. This representation has made the ordinary people of the Northeast more participative and aspirational in our national politics. This augurs well for the youth of Arunachal Pradesh and the Northeast.

Jai Hind!

3

TRANSFORMING THE LAND OF THE RISING SUN

Pema Khandu

When I came to Delhi in the mid-1990s to pursue my graduation at Hindu College, I was amazed by the vast difference between the two worlds that existed in Delhi and Arunachal Pradesh. While Delhi was full of opportunities, Arunachal was spending days in darkness, metaphorically and literally. Several areas did not have electricity for days. The state was grappling with a complete dearth of employment opportunities. Things had been this way since Independence with only marginal improvement. The only wish I had in those days was to see a better, brighter Arunachal during my lifetime.

As destiny would have it, in 2016 I got the opportunity to be the Chief Minister (CM) of Arunachal Pradesh when I was only 36. I knew I had age on my side. By now, both my dreams and ambitions have increased. I did not just want to bridge Arunachal's infrastructure and governance deficit but also wanted Arunachal to be a model state for others. Just like the sun first rises in Arunachal and then reaches other parts of India, I wanted Arunachal to be a leader and a beacon of light for the rest of the country. I started working on a war footing on five key areas: infrastructure, digital governance, social inclusion, hydropower and the cultural mainstreaming of the state. Our sleepless nights and relentless hard work were wholeheartedly supported by Prime Minister (PM) Narendra Modi. The Arunachal dream was his too. No other PM ever had any vision for the Northeast; they seemed happily turned away from the region. Modiji has a distinct vision, political will and a selfless zeal to uplift the Northeast by coordinating the developments to keep them at par with the rest of the country. The entire Northeast region has been immensely benefitted by having a mentor in PM Modi.

Infrastructure Development

As I look back, from 2016, the most critical factor responsible for keeping us behind for a long time was the lack of infrastructure in the state. This was where I had begun my journey. Eleven crucial achievements in the transformation of infrastructure have been a big game changer for the state and improved our standard of living.

Roadways

A total of 50,555 km of road has been built in Arunachal Pradesh, marking a 64 per cent increase in the last seven years from 30,692 km in 2016.[1] The pace of road construction also increased by more than nine times, averaging nearly 2,838 km per year, significantly higher than the average of 300 km of road built in the previous 70 years.[2]

In the same seven-year period since 2016, Arunachal Pradesh has recorded a 65 per cent increase in road density from 36.65 km to 60.36 km per 100 sq. km, which is a good indicator and booster of increased economic activity.[3]

---

[1]Kumar, Pradeep, 'Response to China's Expansionist Policy | BRO Builds 507-Km Roads in Arunachal', *Arunachal Observer*, 7 August 2023, https://tinyurl.com/4v6jtbh6. Accessed on 11 September 2023.

[2]'Arunachal Achievement Booklet 2023', *anyflip*, https://tinyurl.com/26xmvxtj. Accessed on 24 September 2023.

[3]Ibid.

In the last seven years, National Highways (NH) have grown by 138 per cent, of which 2,482 km of NH have been constructed in Arunachal Pradesh.[4] To give an infrastructural push, an additional ₹44,000 crore was granted by the Ministry of Road Transport and Highways (MoRTH) to build 2,574 km of National Highway in the next five years, for which I remain grateful to our dynamic Road Transport and Highways Minister Nitin Gadkari.[5] Two critical national highways have been commissioned in Arunachal Pradesh—the Arunachal Frontier Highway and the Trans-Arunachal Highway (TAH), whereas a major portion of the 1,500 km Trans-Arunachal Highway project is already completed.[6]

Simultaneously, road connectivity has been extended to two of the state's remotest administrative circles, i.e., Vijoynagar on the Indo-Myanmar border and Tali on the Indo-Tibetan border, which have been unconnected since Independence. I personally travel a lot across the length and breadth of Arunachal by road. I feel that it the best way to gauge the state's progress first-hand. If I may humbly add here, it was a personal expedition of mine on this route that acquainted me with the severity of the crisis that resulted from poor infrastructure. I went out of my way to expedite this technically challenging 150-km-long road project.

Our state government inaugurated a record-breaking 365 physical infrastructure projects during the Golden Jubilee year period between 20 January 2022 and 20 January 2023.[7] One of the biggest challenges in a mountainous region is reducing the

---

[4]'Arunachal Pradesh's Leap Towards Advancement', *MyGov*, https://tinyurl.com/3c8css4f. Accessed on 24 September 2023.

[5]'Three Highways Worth Rs 44,000 Crore Approved in Arunachal Pradesh', *Projects Today*, 31 July 2023, https://tinyurl.com/ms25xzz7. Accessed on 11 September 2023.

[6]Subhashini, V. Bhagya, 'Centre Approves 1500-Km Arunachal Pradesh Frontier Highway along LAC: Chief Minister Pema Khandu', *#Swarajya*, 30 November 2022, https://tinyurl.com/mtp6t3um. Accessed on 24 September 2023.

[7]For this and other figures for which no separate source has been provided, the information has been drawn from sources privy to the chief minister's office.

time taken to travel short distances separated by water bodies. In the last seven years, Arunachal Pradesh has been able to connect several regions by building river bridges—notably the motorable steel cable suspension bridge over Siang River, steel arch bridge over Kurung River and Yamne River, double-lane RCC bridge over Tirap River, arch bridge over Poma River, RCC Bridge over Sille River and steel-suspension bridge over Pare River.

As far as urban infrastructure goes, we commissioned the first-ever underpass in Itanagar successfully, and this has been greatly instrumental in lowering traffic congestion in the city and its surrounding areas. Under the Capital Road Improvement Plan, the government has constructed approximately 152 km of road. The fair riding road network of Itanagar Capital Region (ICR) has increased to 45 per cent in 2022–23 and will reach 63 per cent in 2023–24.

Together with the Border Roads Organization (BRO) and the National Highways & Infrastructure Development Corporation Ltd (NHIDCL), Arunachal Pradesh is constructing around 2,000 lane kilometres per year. This has enabled 252 habitations to be connected with the construction of 2,506 km roads in border areas in the last few years. Simultaneously, five infrastructure projects have been taken up by BRO in Arunachal Pradesh, out of which the strategically important Sela and Nechiphu Tunnels will be completed this year.

Under the National Master Plan (NMP) portal, over 26 mandatory data layers have been mapped, and the PM Gati Shakti Data Centre has been established in Itanagar.

Airways

Just like the road infrastructure turnaround, Arunachal's air infrastructure transformation has been equally impressive. The state made a landmark achievement by making the airport at Pasighat in East Siang operational in May 2018. The inauguration of the first greenfield Donyi Polo Airport at Hollongi, Itanagar, in November 2022 has connected the state capital to the rest of the country (currently Mumbai, Delhi, Kolkata and Guwahati). The Pasighat, Tezu and Ziro airports are connected through civil commercial operations.

The state now has seven operational Advanced Landing Grounds (ALG) in Vijoynagar (Changlang District), Walong (Anjaw District), Tuting (Upper Siang District), Ziro (Lower Subansiri District), Aalo (West Siang District), Pasighat (East Siang District) and Mechukha (Shi Yomi District). Three ALGs, namely Mechuka, Tuting and Walong are ready for civil commercial flight operations. Some of our elders who have witnessed the adversities faced by our people during the 1962 Indo-China War cannot imagine the state having so many airports. They cannot thank PM Modi enough for this exceptional turnaround.

Recently, Arunachal Pradesh was awarded the 'Best Emerging State in Aviation Sector' in the country in the Wings India 2022 conference. Our aviation advancement does not stop here. Two more ALGs have been proposed by the state in Anini and Dirang for augmenting intra-state air connectivity under the PM-DevINE scheme. Two Dornier 228 aircraft are taken on lease by the Alliance Air Aviation Ltd from the Hindustan Aeronautics Ltd for exclusive operations in Arunachal Pradesh. Meanwhile, 25 helipads are currently operational in Arunachal Pradesh and the development of 6 heliports is sanctioned under the Regional Connectivity Scheme (RCS-UDAN).[8]

Railways

Arunachal Pradesh was put on the national railway map as Naharlagun was connected with rest of country by broad gauge passenger train service in 2018. The railway station is connected to Guwahati (Donyi Polo Express and Shatabdi Express), New Delhi (Arunachal Express) and Tinsukia (Naharlagun–Tinsukia

---

[8]PTI, 'Twenty-Five Helipads Operational in Arunachal Pradesh: CM', *Outlook*, 13 July 2023, https://tinyurl.com/bdxywu9y. Accessed on 11 September 2023.

Express) by regular service. The Naharlagun station has also been identified for development under the Amrit Bharat Station Scheme with a long-term approach.

In Arunachal Pradesh railways, Passenger Reservation System (PRS) and free Wi-Fi were provided at all stations, along with the Unreserved Ticketing System (UTS) and POS (point of sale) machines at two stations during 2016–22. Work on the proposed world-class Pasighat railway station (6,000 sq. m) is targeted for completion in March 2024.

Meanwhile, Indian Railways has launched 'North East Discovery: Beyond Guwahati', a specially designed tour to cover the Northeastern states of India by Bharat Gaurav Deluxe AC Tourist train. The first state-of-the-art premium luxury coaches connecting Itanagar to Shillong, Tezu, Guwahati, Roing and Namsai were launched in 2022. I remain grateful to our dynamic Railways Minister Ashwini Vaishnav for this wonderful gesture.

Digital Governance

For a mountainous state like Arunachal Pradesh, where travelling from a border district to the state capital can take immense time and effort, digital governance has been a huge boon for government officials. In fact, even for common citizens, the adoption of digital technology and Direct Benefit Transfer (DBT) has enabled them to receive money directly in their accounts without going anywhere. From the time PM Modi launched the Digital India initiative in 2015, I was very keen to optimize its execution in Arunachal. Ever since I became the CM in 2016, digital governance has been one of my key focus areas for the state.

The state government had marked the year 2022–23 as the 'Year of e-Governance' by introducing 22 digital initiatives. At the time of writing, 19 out of 22 initiatives have been implemented, leading to faster and more efficient delivery of G2C, G2G and

G2B services[9], and enhanced transparency and accountability.[10] To personally monitor the execution of digital governance initiatives in real time, I make optimal use of the CM Dashboard, e-Seva Portal, Jansunwai, e-DBT, e-Pragati and e-Inner Line Permit (eILP), which are some of the marquee e-governance projects in the state.

Arunachal Pradesh has been a pioneer in adopting e-governance modules across 772 offices and is perhaps the only Indian state to achieve 100 per cent e-Office implementation in the Civil Secretariat, all district headquarters and directorates. Arunachal Pradesh ranks first among the Northeastern states in terms of e-Office usage, whereby over 28 lakh files have been handled and moved electronically across the offices. Other critical digital modules, such as e-Cabinet, e-Assembly and e-Pragati have also been fully commissioned, providing an end-to-end ICT (Information and communication technology) solution for coordination within departments. The adoption of e-Vidhan and e-Akbari has earned recognition for improving speed, transparency and accountability in governance, reforms and collections.

The e-Pragati portal has been launched for seamless review of project and scheme implementation with districts and various implementation agencies. As many as 26 review meetings have been conducted till date with over 650 agenda items, where construction and maintenance of over 15,500 km of roads, implementation status of over 320 major infrastructure projects and status of installation of over 750 new 4G telecom towers were reviewed by me and my team.

One of the key utilities of our digital governance impetus

---

[9]'Annual Budget 2023-24 Speech of Chowna Mein, Deputy Chief Minister & Minister-In-Charge, Finance, Planning & Investment', *Governtment of Arunachal Pradesh*, 7 March 2023, https://tinyurl.com/54kkta84. Accessed on 6 December 2023.

[10]Mehta, Yuvraj, 'Arunachal CM Launches Online Services under E-Governance Plan', *India Today NE*, 4 May 2023, https://tinyurl.com/2utp6pe8. Accessed on 11 September 2023.

has been the compact monitoring of the Centrally Sponsored Schemes (CSS), which we do through the CSS Tracker in order to achieve 100 per cent saturation. A satellite-based monitoring system has been set up to monitor progress, detect mismatches of funds and send reports regularly for infrastructure projects. Space technology is being extensively used for submergence studies, identifying areas suitable for horticulture crops, and so on. The North East Space Application Centre (NESAC), Shillong has been engaged for the use of space technology in 36 projects.

Our e-Service portal has been launched in all districts to provide 18 services such as ST Certificate, Public Relations (PR) Certificate, Income Certificate, Dependent Certificate, Temporary Resident (TR) Certificate and Marriage Certificate, among others.

The eILP programme launched in November 2022 has earned national repute and bagged two awards at the national level for 'the best government to citizen-centric service application'. The marquee IT initiative has been studied by the Sikkim delegation for replication. In slightly over a year, more than 100,000 ILPs have been generated online, boosting tourism and business travel in the state.

Our digital governance has also improved the ease of life for our citizens. More than 800 pensioners have been issued Digital Life Certificates through the Jeevan Pramaan portal in the state. More than 5,679 pension cases (96 per cent) have been resolved by 'Centralized Information and Pensioner Employees Management system' software developed in mission mode.

The Arunachal Pradesh state government has made it mandatory for all beneficiary-oriented schemes to be onboarded on the Public Finance Management Systems (PFMS). Currently, funds released under 273 central and 10 state schemes are tracked on PFMS.

Table 1
State Schemes Tracked on PFMS

e-Pragati	26 meetings were held to review: Over 650 agenda items Over 15,500 km of road Over 320 large infrastructure projects Over 750 new 4G telecom towers
e-office	Over 28 lakh files handled online, first e-office implementation in the Northeastern region
e-HRMS	Approximately 46 per cent state government employee data migrated in the last one year
Sparrow	Approximately 100 per cent Annual Performance Assessment Report (APAR) for Group A and B employees submitted online
Jansamvad	Over 37,000 minutes of feedback calls were made to beneficiaries of CMAAY and Chief Minister's Relief Fund (CMRF)
e-Services	100,222 certificates generated across 15 services
Ease of Doing Business	505 certificates and licenses issues online
e-Inner Line Permits	191,089 ILPs generated online

Social Inclusion

My third important focus area as CM has been to optimize the impact of the central government's social inclusion schemes. Under PM Modi's vision of 'Sabka Saath, Sabka Vikas, Sabka Vishwas', Sabka Prayaas, the central government has launched some of the finest social inclusion schemes. As CM, I have strived to ensure that not a single resident of Arunachal is deprived of those benefits. Having lived in a remote village while growing up in Tawang district, I know the crucial difference that these social welfare schemes are making in people's lives. Let me, therefore, quickly acquaint you with some of our key achievements in this area.

A total of 1,046 regular camps and 26 mega camps benefitting 11.86 lakh people were conducted as part of the 'Sarkar Aapke Dwar' initiative to provide services to citizens at their doorstep. Following its success, the revamped 'Seva Aapke Dwar 2.0' was launched in October 2022 and has covered over 182,965 beneficiaries through 237 camps. The emphasis is on bottom-up micro planning to attain saturation of priority schemes of the government and provide beneficiary-oriented services in the camps.

Financial Inclusion

In order to increase financial inclusion and social security coverage under the Pradhan Mantri Jeevan Jyoti Bima Yojana (PMJJBY) and Pradhan Mantri Suraksha Bima Yojana (PMSBY), our government has decided to pay the insurance premium for contingency workers, casual labourers and ALCs aged between 18 and 50 years working in the government sector. The state government is also paying the premium under these two schemes for all Anganwadi workers, mid-day meal workers, auxiliary nurse midwives and *gaon buras*.

A total of 107,346 registered subscribers have been covered with a life insurance cover of ₹2 lakh under PMJJBY, whereas 44,151 subscribers have been covered under the Atal Pension Yojana as of 31 May 2023.

Now, let us come to the National Food Security Act (NFSA)—one of the key enablers in fighting poverty. The state government has so far covered nearly 8.5 lakh beneficiaries, improving food accessibility for citizens under the NFSA. To further support the economic and social wellbeing of the people, all the beneficiaries are availing free food grains as decided by the Government of India (GoI) with effect from 1 January 2023. As of March 2023, a total of more than 4.5 lakh metric tonnes of free rice grains have been distributed to nearly 8.4 lakh beneficiaries[11] at 5 kg per person per month under the successful Pradhan Mantri Garib Kalyan Anna Yojana to the remotest villages in a time-bound manner.

Another path-breaking step has been the implementation of the One Nation One Ration Card Scheme due to which 1,968 fair price shops (FPS)[12] in the State have been automated, resulting in about 1.8 lakh ration cards being automated with EPOS (electronic point of sale) devices, increasing the availability and accessibility of services for all citizens, including those residing outside the state.

The state currently supports over 48,722 elderly beneficiaries, over 7,168 widow beneficiaries and nearly 3,435 disability beneficiaries under the National Social Assistance Programme (NSAP). I am happy to inform that the top-up given by the state government to each beneficiary under the NSAP for old age, widow and disability pension is much more than the central allocation given by the GoI.

Now, let us talk about two of the key flagship programmes of PM Modi's government. In order to provide affordable housing to all under the Pradhan Mantri Awas Yojana-Gramin (PMAY-G), 36,378 pucca houses have been sanctioned and 13,744 houses have been constructed. The Chief Minister Rural Housing Scheme (CMRHS) provides a top-up of ₹20,000 to each eligible beneficiary.[13]

---

[11]'Annual Budget 2023-24 Speech of Chowna Mein, Deputy Chief Minister & Minister-In-Charge, Finance, Planning & Investment', *Governtment of Arunachal Pradesh*, 7 March 2023, https://tinyurl.com/54kkta84. Accessed on 6 December 2023.

[12]*National Food Security Portal*, https://tinyurl.com/f3tj2v2b. Accessed on 11 September 2023.

[13]'Arunachal Pradesh-Ushering Development by Uplifting Rural Livelihoods', *MyGov*, 14 July 2023, https://tinyurl.com/yux8uzeu. Accessed on 11 September 2023.

Employment

Under the Mahatma Gandhi National Rural Employment Guarantee Act (MGNREGA), around 3.11 lakh job cards were issued till date in Arunachal Pradesh, providing at least one hundred days of guaranteed wage employment to households in rural areas.[14] Over 85,000 women were mobilized into 9,301 self-help groups (SHGs) across the state, which are critical for women's empowerment and the growth of the rural economy. Under the Arunachal State Rural Livelihood Mission (ArSLM), the state has formed and trained over 1,100 SHGs and opened more than 60,000 savings bank accounts, enabling a credit linkage of over 2,900 SHGs. Furthermore, the state government has extended support to 500 SHGs under the Arun Shree Rinn Yojana with a fixed deposit of ₹1 lakh each to be maintained in their bank accounts. These groups will be able to issue loans against the said deposit to boost their livelihoods.

Under the Pradhan Mantri Formalisation of Micro food processing Enterprises (PMFME) scheme, 1,081 SHG members have set up over 164 group enterprises. Similarly, 240 Mother's Kitchens have been established by women SHG members with financial support from ArSLM, along with one Mother's Collective setup to provide market access to products by SHGs.

Healthcare

Under Chief Minister Arogya Arunachal Yojana (CMAAY), together with Ayushman Bharat Pradhan Mantri Jan Arogya Yojana (AB PM-JAY), more than 1.3 lakh families have been covered to provide cashless healthcare assurance of up to ₹5 lakh to the indigenous people of the state. Under the two schemes, 25,000 patients have been treated, with a cumulative spending of ₹39 crore. More than 90 hospitals are participating in the scheme,

---

[14]Ibid.

of which 28 are hospitals outside the state. Launched in 2019, free diagnostics service is implemented in 55 health facilities at present where 44 indicated tests are performed to reduce out of pocket expenditure. About 25 lakh tests have been conducted benefiting more than eight lakh patients.

Women and Child Development

Our state government has been equally proactive in doing its bit for women and children. An additional ₹5,000 has been provided as fixed deposit over and above the existing ₹20,000 for the 8,371 girl child born (beneficiaries) in Arunachal Pradesh under the 'Dulari Kanya Scheme'. In order to recognize women achievers, Arunachal Pradesh provides ₹20 lakh per year for undertaking exposure visits and educational tours of rural women.

The Ministry of Tribal Affairs has sanctioned a total of 12 Eklavya Model Residential Schools (EMRS) for the state. Out of these, three have been inaugurated this year and two more are on the verge of completion. Fifty dedicated girls' residential schools named Kasturba Gandhi Balika Vidyalaya (KGBV) have been established in the state, along with 38 KGBVs attached to higher secondary schools.

In 2018, the government of Arunachal Pradesh launched the POSHAN Abhiyaan (erstwhile National Nutrition Mission) to address malnutrition in the state. A total of 10,939 activities were conducted in the 26 districts that delivered improvements in outcomes of stunting, undernutrition, low birth weight in children, anemia and women's nutrition. Arunachal Pradesh was ranked sixth among all states in India for performance in POSHAN KPIs (key performance indicators), according to India Policy Insights (IPI). Around 98 Integrated Child Development Services (ICDS) projects were made operational in Arunachal Pradesh. Under the supplementary nutrition programme (SNP), approximately 1.8 lakh pregnant women, lactating mothers and children under six years of age were provided nutrition to bridge the gap between the Recommended Dietary Allowance (RDA) and the Average Daily Intake (ADI). The programme has also been expanded to cover more remote and underserved areas of the state.

Under Pradhan Mantri Ujjwala Yojana and Ujjwala 2.0, 48,503 LPG (liquefied petroleum gas) connections were provided to BPL (below poverty line) beneficiaries in Arunachal Pradesh as a measure of relief for women who toil for firewood every day. The state government provides an additional top-up subsidy of ₹1,000 to each BPL household over the ₹1,600 given by the GoI.

The humanitarian CM Baal Sewa Scheme has been launched to support children orphaned due to Covid-19 through the provision of cash incentives. The PM CARES for Children Scheme is also being implemented in the state for the rehabilitation of Covid-19 orphaned children. The Arunachal Pradesh Scheme for providing grants for medical treatment of children with special needs residing in Child Care Institutes was notified in 2020.

Hydropower

While social equality and inclusiveness must be our first priority, that should not prevent us from harnessing the true potential of the state. In a state rich in natural resources and water bodies, there is immense potential to generate hydropower. Unconventional sources of energy production ease the burden of producing electricity through age-old methods, while also being environment-friendly.

Prime Minister Modi has been striving to make India an energy surplus country. I cannot think of any other PM who has been so particular about the equitable distribution of energy. It gives me a lot of pride to share Arunachal's achievements in the hydropower sector, bolstered by the support of the central government.

In a span of seven years, the installed capacity in the state saw a tremendous increase (213 per cent) from 405 MW in financial year (FY) 2015–16 to 1,270 MW in FY 2022–23.[15] The recently inaugurated 600 MW Kameng Hydro Power project made Arunachal Pradesh the second power surplus state in Northeast region. In a major national infrastructure push, the Dibang Multipurpose Project of 2,880 MW (largest project of the country till date) has been approved by the GoI in February 2023 with an estimated outlay of ₹31,876 crore. Expected benefits, thereby, are estimated to be 12 per cent free power approximating ₹560 crore per annum and additional one per cent free power for Local Area Development Fund equivalent to ₹47 crore per year.[16]

The Ministry of Power, GoI, has approved the proposal we made to rejuvenate 29 stalled hydropower projects by assigning such projects to Central Public Sector Undertakings, namely National Hydroelectric Power Corporation (NHPC), North Eastern Electric Power Corporation Limited (NEEPCO), Satluj Jal Vidyut Nigam (SJVN) and Tehri Hydro Development Corporation Limited (THDCIL). The total installed capacity of these projects is 32,415 MW. Six Projects of Etalin, Tato I & II, Heo, Nafra and Kamala with combined 6,063 MW potential have been prioritized in Phase One.[17]

Cultural Mainstreaming

While the physical distance between the Northeast and other parts of the country has been bridged by speedy infrastructure creation, a bigger task was to culturally unite the region with the rest of the

---

[15]'Annual Budget 2023-24 Speech of Chowna Mein, Deputy Chief Minister & Minister-In-Charge, Finance, Planning & Investment', *Governtment of Arunachal Pradesh*, 7 March 2023, https://tinyurl.com/54kkta84. Accessed on 6 December 2023.

[16]Ibid.

[17]'Mein, Singh Discuss Harnessing Arunachal's Hydropower Potential', *The Arunachal Times*, 23 November 2022, https://tinyurl.com/42rkzfck. Accessed on 6 December 2023.

country. For this, the credit again goes to PM Modi. His entire mission of 'Ek Bharat, Shreshtha Bharat' is based on invoking age-old confluences between diverse regions. For the people of Arunachal Pradesh, this was a new experience. No other PM has in the past shown so much interest in culturally integrating the people of the Northeast with other parts of the country.

In a historic event in May 2023, PM Modi interacted with the members of community-based organizations (CBOs), representing 26 tribes of Arunachal Pradesh. The CBO members also engaged in exposure visits, knowledge sharing and interaction sessions on the trip to the Statue of Unity, GIFT City, Pradhanmantri Sangrhalay and Rashtrapati Bhavan, among others.

Under the 'Ek Bharat Shreshtha Bharat' programme, Arunachal Pradesh partnered with Meghalaya and Uttar Pradesh to enhance interaction and promote mutual understanding between people of different states and Union Territories. Many cultural exchanges were held in this regard, including vlogging and culinary exchange events at Mangalmay Institute of Engineering and Technology, Greater Noida and Institute of Hotel Management (IHM), Shillong respectively.

During the Madhavpur Ghed fair held at Madhavpur in Gujarat during 10–14 April 2022, along with the participation of artists and artisans from the eight Northeastern states, 84 persons from the state of Arunachal Pradesh attended the event as part of the family of Rani Rukmini. For our younger generation, it was an overwhelming moment. While we were growing up, times were different. We were seldom told about Arunachal's role in the ancient past and the part it played in the inspiring Krishna–Rukmini story. Today's younger generation is growing up rooted and well-informed about our religious and spiritual history.

There are other steps that we have taken to ensure that our school children grow up imbibing the best influences. In order to ensure that our children are rooted in the state's culture and traditions, we have developed books on folk tales from eight local tribes (Nyishi, Galo, Tagin, Wanchoo, Tangsa, Idu Mishmi, Taroan Mishmi and Kaman Mishmi) as supplementary reading material for primary school students. The names of 222 war heroes from Arunachal Pradesh, which include 19 unsung heroes, 76 martyrs and 127 freedom fighters, were recorded and documented. Furthermore, these unsung heroes were posthumously awarded with a citation and medallion on the thirty-seventh Statehood Day. An exhibition on the lives and contributions of our unsung heroes was inaugurated by the Hon'ble President of India. A list of 15 'Unsung Heroes' was submitted to GoI for national recognition.

In recent years, the Research Institute of World's Ancient Traditions, Cultures and Heritage (RIWATCH) has emerged as a leading cultural research institute linking vibrant and living 'cultures' with sustainable prosperity. Arunachal Pradesh also inaugurated a unique museum established by RIWATCH in 2017.

Last but not the least, an online digital platform, e-Indigenous Culture Portal, having folklore and folk music of all major tribes is being built by the state government.

In this brief article, I have tried to provide a glimpse of the multifaceted developmental journey our state has been undertaking under the guidance of PM Narendra Modi. I take this opportunity to invite all the readers to our beautiful state. Come as a tourist and be our guest, experience our beautiful state. You might fall in love with the place and want to live here. I feel humbled to be a part of this historic transition of the state from a quiet corner to the heart of India.

Jai Hind! Jai Arunachal!

4

NURTURING INDIA'S SWITZERLAND OF THE EAST

Yanthungo Patton

The Northeastern states have a significant place in the history of India. The Ahoms of Assam (known as Kamrupa in earlier times) defeated the mighty Mughals with the support of chieftains from the hills at the banks of the Brahmaputra River in 1671. The Burmese invasion of Assam between 1817 and 1826 was time and again fought off fiercely by the frontline natives of the hills. The resident tribes still recall the horrific tales from the times when the Assam territory came under the control of Burma (1821–1825). Imphal and Kohima (the state capital) witnessed the Japanese aggression upon India under the command of General Kotoku Sato during one of the toughest wars in the history of mankind. The World War II was put to a stop at the Battle of Kohima in 1944. Such invasions and the resultant sufferings have impacted the social demography of the Northeast. The neglect of the Indian political machinery alienated the region and its narratives from the mainstream attention of the country for a long period of time, creating frustration and hostility among its people.

Since 2014, Northeast India has been closely nurtured by Prime Minister (PM) Narendra Modi, and the growth of the region has been planned with special interest. On three important occasions, PM Modi has come to Nagaland and interacted with the residents of the state, unlike former PM Manmohan Singh, who never did so.

Historic initiatives under the BJP government's Act East Policy (AEP) were launched at the 12th ASEAN[1]-India Summit held in Myanmar to strengthen the North Eastern Region (NER) through economic cooperation, cultural ties, improved connectivity and capacity expansion in order to promote a strategic relationship with other Southeast Asian nations. Artificial boundaries with other parts of the country have now been broken and the bridges of prosperity and progress are making their way into the region. Gigantic projects have been sanctioned and more are in the pipeline—micro and macro programmes under them will impact the region both in the short and long run. The efforts of the Bharatiya Janata Party (BJP) government are being channelled to honour the trust of the people and support their prosperous dreams.

'The results of Northeast (of India) is not only about less distance between hearts but also the reflection of a new ideology.'[2] These words of PM Modi aptly define the developmental vision behind the transformation of the eight Northeastern states. Today, the entire belt experiences palpable change in terms of peace and progress. This energizes a remote state like Nagaland even more because of the multiplicity of opportunities for hidden potential and suppressed talent.

The government, under the current dispensation, has worked diligently to understand and address the issues in Nagaland. A selection of the distinct areas of transformation are listed below.

Law and Order Vis-à-Vis Naga Issues

For more than seven and a half decades, Nagaland has been in the limelight for insurgency-related issues. The central government,

---

[1]Association of Southeast Asian Nations

[2]'Northeast Poll Results: Some Say "Mar Ja Modi" While Others Want "Mat Ja Modi", Says PM at Victory Address', *The Economic Times*, 2 March 2023, https://tinyurl.com/yyzhvtr8. Accessed on 24 September 2023.

led by PM Atal Bihari Vajpayee, took up the matter with all seriousness, but work halted soon after the former PM vacated his office. Prime Minister Modi has returned to the incomplete tasks with renewed vigour, handling the situation diplomatically while recognizing the unique Naga history and culture.

The Centre is seriously engaged in a meaningful and responsible dialogue with the National Socialist Council of Nagaland-Isak-Muivah (NSCN-IM) and Naga National Political Groups (NNPGs). The willingness to resolve the problems and the patience to understand the pain points are raising trust, thereby putting an end to a long struggle for political and social self-determination. The law and order situation in the state has improved tremendously over the past 10 years. Recently, Nagaland has been voted as the 'best performing small state' in law and order among other small states by The India Today Group State of the States survey.[3] The Armed Forces (Special Powers) Act (AFSPA) of 1958 has been lifted from 18 police stations while it continues to be operational in some areas under some relaxations.[4] The Nagaland police force is well-equipped to deal with modern issues like cybercrime, net terrorism and other tech-related crimes, apart from other law and order issues.

Education and Vocational Training

During the last decade, tremendous development has taken place in the field of education. While Nagaland is ranked among the states with the highest literacy rates in the country, the scope for specializations and higher education is relatively low. With the introduction of the National Education Policy (NEP) founded

[3]'Nagaland Awarded Best Small State in "Law & Order"', *Nagaland Post*, 22 November 2019, https://tinyurl.com/bdhhvdda. Accessed on 12 September 2023.
[4]'Centre Reduces Number of Places under AFSPA in the Northeast', *Hindustan Times*, 26 March 2023, https://tinyurl.com/5n7swnzm. Accessed on 12 September 2023.

on the four formidable pillars of *Access, Equity, Quality* and *Accountability*, fresh avenues have been generated for the students. Their pursuit of skills and a career of their choice has been made easier with better resources, connectivity and institutions available for counselling, training and channelling their talent. Exhaustive consultations and deliberations have been conducted with the grassroots in the education sector, along with urban and non-resident Indian (NRI) experts. Meaningful collaborations have enhanced access to education, particularly in the remote corners and among the disadvantaged sections of Naga society.

Secondary and higher secondary education have been successfully modernized with a focus on experiential learning to develop skills like critical thinking and problem solving. Sincere efforts are being made to streamline the disciplines of arts and sciences with equal emphasis and establish a productive balance between curricular and extracurricular activities.

Recently, the government notification[5] delinking higher secondary (+2) from degree colleges has been welcomed by the All Nagaland Private Schools' Association (ANPSA). The NEP 2020 recommends schooling to follow the 5+3+3+4 structure, taking into account the pre-primary years of schooling as well. Some colleges have been given autonomous status, which translates into better infrastructure, modern courses, updated teaching methodologies and qualified resources. New universities have also been approved and recognized. A new medical college has come up in Kohima and has commenced the academic session in 2023. Medical colleges in Mon are also coming up, while Ayush colleges are earmarked in the state. The Nagaland Ayush Counselling 2023 will be conducted based on the National Eligibility cum Entrance Test (NEET) score. The Directorate of Technical Education, Kohima, will conduct online counselling

[5]'ANPSA Welcomes Delinking of Class 11 & 12 from Degree Colleges', *The Morung Express*, 14 May 2022, https://tinyurl.com/5xr99df8. Accessed on 24 September 2023.

by using the NEET result/scorecard. A full-fledged engineering college is in the offing, while several polytechnic colleges are functioning satisfactorily.

For a holistic and multidisciplinary development of the learners, vocational education is being integrated with general education. The NEP aims to ensure that every child learns at least one vocational subject and is exposed to several more from Class 6 onward. This would lead to emphasizing the dignity of labour and relevant skill-building for self-sustenance. The goal of the policy is to have at least 50 per cent of the learners receive vocational education by 2025. Vocational training in the fields of music, handicrafts, animal husbandry, masonry, electricity and solar lights, tourism and hotel management is being imparted, which has shown promising results. The PM's flagship programmes, Sarva Siksha Abhiyan (SSA), Samagra Siksha[6] and Nagaland: Enhancing Classroom Teaching and Resources[7] (NECTAR), are a success story in Nagaland.

Rural Development and Livelihood

The larger population of Nagaland lives in villages. Nagaland is a land of villages with a unique form of a republic. The backbone of its rural economy is agriculture and its allied occupations include beekeeping, weaving, handicrafts, basketry and fishing, among others. Through the noble initiative of PM Modi, the National Rural Livelihood Mission (NRLM) and its sister project of the State

[6]The Sarva Siksha Abhiyaan (SSA) scheme is designed to improve the curriculum, educational planning, teacher education and management. Samagra Shiksha scheme is an integrated scheme for compulsory and quality school education for children from diverse background, multilingual needs and academic abilities with an equitable and inclusive classroom environment covering the entire gamut from pre-school to Class 12.

[7]Nagaland: Enhancing Classroom Teaching and Resources–A project to enhance the governance of schools and improve teaching practices and learning environment in selected school complexes.

Mission, NSRLM (Nagaland State Rural Livelihood Mission), the living standards of the rural populace are alleviated. The NSRLM works in 1,241 villages under 74 RD blocks across 11 districts, with the aim of creating effective and efficient institutional platforms to enable the rural poor to increase their household income by means of sustainable livelihood enhancements and better access to financial services.[8] Each village has several self-help groups (SHGs), comprising 20–30 members. These groups set a target for every calendar year, which in turn helps the community and the group grow through marketing and making profits out of it.

With so many activities at hand, the regions are evolving into aspirational villages, uplifted in specific development parameters like health and nutrition, education, agriculture and water resources, financial inclusion, skill development and basic infrastructure under the National Institution for Transforming India (NITI) Aayog's flagship Aspirational District Programme (ADP) 2023 initiative. Skill development has also helped both the educated and the uneducated find ways for imparting training and giving job placement wherever possible. This has considerably helped in streamlining the youths towards self-reliance. The Prime Minister's Employment Generation Programme (PMEGP) has also helped in assisting the economically weak to set up businesses and upgrade through microfinance.

Medical and Healthcare

Medical facilities and healthcare have improved in the state. To help cater to the needs of the patients, the state government is taking concrete steps to bring drastic changes to the system. The Kohima Medical College, with its intake of 100 students, has benefitted the students and the residents of the state. There is a need for more healthcare workers, especially after the Covid-19

[8]*Nagaland State Rural Livelihoods Mission*, http://tinyurl.com/yk22ndwd. Accessed on 12 September 2023.

pandemic. Many more medical and Ayush hospitals are coming up in different districts with the support of the central government. The Christian Institute of Health Sciences and Research (CISHR) located in Dimapur, has recently been upgraded to a standardized unit. The Chief Minister's Health Insurance Scheme (CMHIS) will cover the costs of treatment for citizens—both government servants and retired.

Roads and Railways

Nagaland faces the challenges of a hilly terrain, making accessibility difficult in many places, especially during the monsoons. Prime Minister Modi's government is especially attentive towards this lack of accessibility and has initiated the connectivity revolution. Significant improvements have been registered with the support of the central government, while a lot of work is still in progress. The 14.71 km-long four-lane highway on NH 29 from Dimapur to Kohima, under the Ministry of Road Transport and Highways (MoRTH) is nearing completion despite numerous challenges like frequent unfavourable weather, labour shortage, the Covid-19 pandemic and others. This project will improve the connectivity between the capital city and other major commercial centres in the state, thereby enabling faster movement of people and goods for growth and prosperity. Several national and state highways have been completed.

In terms of international road connectivity, the 1,408 km-long India–Myanmar–Thailand Trilateral Highway (IMT Highway) falls under India's 'Look East Policy' and will connect Moreh in India with Mae Sot in Thailand via Myanmar.[9] The IMT Highway passes through the Northeastern states of Assam, Nagaland and Manipur and will boost trade and commerce in the ASEAN-India

[9]ANI, 'India-Myanmar-Thailand Trilateral Highway: Progress Update', *ETInfra.com*, 20 July 2023, https://tinyurl.com/45mcnuet. Accessed on 8 December 2023.

Free Trade Area (AIFTA). Nagaland got its second railway station at Shokhuvi in August 2022, after a gap of 100 years. This will also establish Manipur's first freight connection passing through Nagaland, thereby bridging the divides. The Zubza railway project, which is to connect the state capital with Dimapur, Shokhuvi and others, is also on the fast track.

Tourism and Hospitality, Sports and Music

Nagaland is a bountiful land with natural scenery. Dubbed by many as the 'Switzerland of the East', it captivates all with its exquisite scenic beauty. Nagaland is known for its famed Dzukou valley and the mighty Doyang river, which flows into the Brahmaputra—whose dam area is a stopover for migratory birds, rendering it the title of the 'falcon capital of the world'. The mystery of Shilloi Lake and many more delights await and beckon tourists. The renowned Hornbill Festival attracts lakhs of both domestic and foreign tourists. We were touched by the presence of PM Modi as the special guest during the opening ceremony of the festival in 2014.

Tourism is a big industry in Nagaland and we have earmarked some potential projects to put Nagaland on the map as the ultimate global tourist destination. The state houses the best brands of hotels with modern amenities for premier and budget occupancy, well-maintained homestays and private inns for a comfortable stay. We are also the second state in the Northeast to introduce tourist police to facilitate their tours. The recently concluded G20 Summit held in Kohima has opened the scope for more direct investors in multidisciplinary sectors, including tourism.

Our culture is distinctively unique and rich with the traditional knowledge system, given the fact that we are located far from the hustle and bustle of mega-metropolitan influences. Our ornaments, handicrafts and hand-woven clothes stand out. So does our folklore, songs and war dances. The customary laws are so sacred that even a grown man would swear not to go against these practices.

Many developments have taken place in the fields of sports and music too. Sports are definitely the mantra for wellness, achievement and discipline. Through generous sanctions from the Centre, we are grooming young sportspersons towards excellence. Nagaland's youth have excelled in the fields of badminton, archery, Sepak takraw, martial arts and wrestling. Khelo India, a Ministry of Sports initiative, has been instrumental in uplifting sports and youth resources in the state.

Music in Nagaland comes naturally, like the sounds of birds from the hills. The state has always been at the forefront of Indian art, with traditional sensibilities marrying modern techniques to entertain audiences near and far. The Task Force for Music and Arts (TaFMA) is further mentoring local talent to compete on national and international platforms.

Water Supply, JJM and Power

In the state, water is scarce throughout the year except during the monsoon season. With the coming of the Jal Jeevan Mission (JJM), almost all villages, even the remotest ones, have water reaching their doorsteps, which is a welcome change for the people. The farmers are no longer worried about water resources while irrigating their fields and orchards; instead, they are concentrating on dreaming bigger and expanding their output from the fields. Nagaland has achieved 52 per cent of the JJM project as of 15 October 2022.[10]

Power supply and connectivity have seen a marked improvement. However, we cannot claim to have achieved complete self-reliance yet. The state needs to generate its own power supply. We rely on power purchases from other states. Recently, a state load despatch centre (SLDC) has been inaugurated at Dimapur

[10]'Training on JJM Project Underway in Wokha', *Eastern Mirror*, 17 October 2022, https://tinyurl.com/enz2aws7. Accessed on 12 September 2023.

and it takes care of the transmission and distribution of power. This controls tariff loss and has, to some extent, stabilized power trading. New and renewable energy is also a supplement for the otherwise power deficit state.

A Visionary Leadership

The people of Nagaland receive the benefits of free food grains, edible oils, pulses and other essential rations. During the Covid-19 pandemic, the central government handled the situation tactfully, which deeply impacted the lives of the people and armed them with physical well-being and financial stability in the long run. The United Nations Development Programme (UNDP), India supported the central government's Covid-19 response by procuring and providing personal protective equipment such as masks, gloves, sanitizers and thermal scanners for use at health facilities in Nagaland.[11] During the second wave of the Covid-19 pandemic, the government made localized arrangements to make up for the lack of healthcare infrastructure, especially in rural areas.[12] Autonomy was granted to the state governments to handle the spread of the virus and deftly control the overwhelmed urban hospitals, which were running beyond capacity and failing under the growing pressure. Old age pension, Mahatma Gandhi National Rural Employment Guarantee Act (MGNREGA) 2005, Post Matric Scholarship (PMS) and other benefits are also availed.

The people of Nagaland have confided their trust in the visionary leadership of PM Modi, which, I am very sure, will go

---

[11]'Need of the Hour: Ensuring Safety of Health Workers to Combat Covid-19', *United Nations Development Programme*, https://tinyurl.com/2vvnwbtu. Accessed on 24 September 2023.

[12]Aomatsung and Temjen Jamir, 'A Study on the Socio-Economic Impact Of Covid 19 in Nagaland', *International Journal of Advance Research and Innovative Ideas in Education*, Vol. 8, No. 2, 2022, https://tinyurl.com/5af663va. Accessed on 24 September 2023.

a long way. All the achievements mentioned above have been made possible with the constant support and encouragement from the central government. A single chapter in a book provides only so much space. However, there is much more to be said about my state. The stories of the achievements of the Naga community are just the tip of the iceberg. Many more will flourish in the days to come.

Let me conclude by saying that no other PM of India has done so much for the Northeastern states as PM Modi has done in the last nine years. He has truly taken his stand in the realm of truth, taking every region of the country and its people on board. His vision of *Sabka Saath, Sabka Vikas, Sabka Vishwas, Sabka Prayaas* has inspired people across all hierarchies and we are tirelessly striving towards bigger stories of growth to make our land proud. Jai Hind!

5

RESOLVING BORDER DISPUTES: A PRECURSOR TO LONGSTANDING PEACE

Gen. V.K. Singh

As the first Development of North Eastern Region (DoNER) minister under Prime Minister (PM) Narendra Modi, I was fortunate to have developed, under the PM's guidance, a master plan for the region's expeditious development. I personally travelled extensively across the belt to take a first-hand account of the deficits that needed immediate addressal. However, a year later, I was assigned another ministry and my immediate involvement with DoNER ended.

Almost eight years later, when I travelled to Nagaland's Mon district in the first week of May 2023 to inspect an ongoing project by the National Highways Authority of India (NHAI), I was very impressed to see the vast strides undertaken in road connectivity. This improvement in the other states of the Northeast is just as palpable. The air connectivity has also been upgraded and the railway projects are on track. This is certainly a discernible display of optimism in the region.

As infrastructure development has been spoken of in great detail, let me focus here on one very crucial aspect that has been a quiet enabler—the Modi government's commitment to resolve the pervasive territorial friction among the Northeastern states.

I will write here with specific reference to the resolution of the long-standing territorial discord between Assam and Arunachal Pradesh, facilitated by the proactive intervention of the central government.

The Land Dispute

To understand the history of the dispute, we need to go back to colonial times. In the year 1873, the Bengal Eastern Frontier Regulations came into effect, which set up an 'inner line' to mark a boundary between the plains and the frontier hills. This boundary later acquired the name North-East Frontier Tracts (NEFT) in 1915. The colonial state intentionally left large, undefined territories in sparsely populated regions as part of its frontier policy. In 1951, a sub-committee, headed by Gopinath Bordoloi, who was serving as the chief minister (CM) of Assam, furnished a report concerning the administration of the North-East Frontier Agency (NEFA) (formerly known as the NEFT), which later became Arunachal Pradesh (incorporating some parts of Assam). According to the recommendations, NEFA transferred approximately 3,648 sq. km of the plain area in Balipara and Sadiya foothills to Assam. However, the stance of Arunachal Pradesh has been unwavering in asserting that the transfer took place without the consent of its populace. They contended that the forested areas of the plains historically fell under the jurisdiction of the tribal hill chiefs. Both the colonial state and the Ahom kings, with whom the tribal chiefs had a 'posa'[1] relationship, recognized their rights over the land and forests.

[1]A system in which the hilly areas were permitted to levy an annual collection of goods and also access the labour service of the Assamese pykes, in return they had to commit to refrain from making inroads into Ahom territory; Theunuo, Thepfusalie, and Rabin Deka, 'Colonial Rule and Agrarian Transformation in Naga Hills: A Socio-Economic View of Angami Society', *Social Change and Development*, 2020, http://tinyurl.com/yc74m9rk. Accessed on 15 December 2023.

There have been several attempts to resolve the border conflict between Assam and Arunachal Pradesh. Back in 1979, both the state governments concurred to form a high-powered committee aimed at addressing the unresolved issues. However, the progress made was scant and sluggish. Furthermore, the Assam government remained silent in the face of Arunachal Pradesh's plea for the return of 956 sq. km of land. In the years 1983–84, approximately 489 sq. km of the border along the north bank of the Brahmaputra river, had been demarcated. Nonetheless, subsequent advancements were impeded by Arunachal Pradesh's refusal to endorse the recommendations.

In 1989, Arunachal Pradesh reasserted its claim, stating that it sought only a modest portion of the plains that had been transferred to Assam. In response, the Government of Assam instigated a legal proceeding in the Supreme Court, seeking clarification on the Assam-Arunachal boundary. The Supreme Court formed a committee headed by retired judge, Justice Tarun Chatterjee. By that time, Arunachal Pradesh had increased its claim from 956 sq. km to 1,119.2 sq. km. In 2007, the Justice Chatterjee Commission, validated nearly 80 per cent of Arunachal Pradesh's claim. However, Assam dismissed the findings in 2009, contending that the boundary matter should be settled through mutual discussion and compromise. In its conclusive 2014 report, the Justice Chatterjee Commission proposed that Arunachal Pradesh regain certain territories transferred in 1951 and advised both states to seek a middle ground through discussions.

Resolving the Issue

It is noteworthy that after an eight-year hiatus, PM Modi and Home Minister Amit Shah recognized the significance of resolving border disputes among the Northeastern states due to their implications on internal and external security. Fortunately, Himanta Biswa Sarma and Pema Khandu, CM of Assam and

Arunachal Pradesh respectively, were from the same political party and were in accord to seek a negotiated settlement. Conversations initiated in January 2022 culminated in the issuance of the Namsai Declaration after the third round of discussions.

Namsai, situated along the border between Assam and Arunachal Pradesh near the Noa Dihing River, was primarily known for its Golden Pagoda, called 'Kongmu Kham' in the Tai-Khamti language. This stands as one of the largest Buddhist monasteries in Northeast India. Meanwhile, the inter-state border covers a distance of 804 km, stretching across eight districts in Assam and twelve districts in Arunachal Pradesh.

The entire process started with the Namsai Declaration on 15 July 2022, when Assam CM Himanta Biswa Sarma and Arunachal Pradesh CM Pema Khandu, met and engaged in extensive deliberations.

Prime Minister Narendra Modi and the Minister of Home Affairs Amit Shah played a significant role in facilitating the resolution process. With deft coordination and planning, they were able to successfully settle the dispute concerning 37 villages, while 12 regional committees comprising officials and public representatives from both states were assigned to handle the remaining villages. These committees conducted physical visits to the disputed areas for an on-ground perspective on the problem. Their recommendations were consequently better informed and insightful.

Both states assessed the advancements made based on the Namsai Declaration. It culminated with the signing of a memorandum of understanding (MoU) between the two CMs with Home Minister Amit Shah in attendance in Delhi, on 20 April 2023. They successfully resolved their differences regarding an additional 34 villages. Of the 71 villages covered in the agreement, 60 will fall under the jurisdiction of Arunachal Pradesh while Assam will oversee 10, with one village being shifted from Arunachal Pradesh to Assam. A continuous dialogue will be held to determine the boundary demarcation of 49 villages out of the remaining 52, within a span of six months. The three remaining villages located partly within the Indian Air Force (IAF) grounds in Dullong, will be under the purview of the Arunachal Pradesh government, working in consultation with the Indian government and the IAF. Moreover, Arunachal Pradesh consented to cede its claim over a substantial portion of disputed land in Jorhat, Assam.[2]

A pivotal cause outlined in the MoU between Arunachal Pradesh and Assam states that no new areas or villages beyond the existing 123 claimed villages would be added. Both state governments also agreed to take effective measures to prevent any new encroachments in the border regions. The peaceful and positive manner in which everything progressed set the right benchmark to settle any civil disputes in the future.

The Modi government has decisively resolved numerous pressing concerns in the Northeastern region. In the course of time, several peace agreements have been signed with various militant organizations, including the National Liberation Front of Tripura (NLFT) in 2019, Bru tribal refugees in 2020, and the Bodo, Karbi and Adivasi groups. Progress has also been made in resolving border disputes between Assam and Meghalaya. Furthermore, Nagaland and Assam have shown a readiness to collaborate on exploring oil resources within the contested region between them, indicating a positive outlook for the region's future. It is becoming increasingly evident that a holistic and equitable development in the region can only be achieved by addressing conflict-inducing issues and prioritizing the well-being of the people over territorial disputes. This people-centric vision of PM Modi has proved its effectiveness in resolving disputes in the Northeastern states or 'Ashta Lakshmi' as he calls them.

---

[2]'Assam-Arunachal Pradesh Sign Border Pact Ending Decades-Old Disputes', *The Economic Times*, 21 April 2023, https://tinyurl.com/y64ampja. Accessed on 18 September 2023.

6

A RESURGENT NORTHEAST

Baijayant Panda

The Northeast region of India has historically faced various challenges, including under-representation in the central government. However, under the leadership of Prime Minister (PM) Narendra Modi, the region has seen a significant increase in its representation in the central government, with the highest-ever number of ministers from the Northeast. This is a testament to the central government's commitment in ensuring inclusivity and regional diversity in decision-making. Their presence is a sign that the region is finally being given the attention it deserves, reflecting the government's commitment to recognize the deserving talents emerging from the Northeast.

Culture

India's Northeast region boasts of a rich cultural heritage and has produced numerous national icons who have made significant contributions to the nation. Lachit Borphukan, an Ahom general from Assam, is revered for his leadership during the Battle of Saraighat against the Mughals. Rani Gaidinliu, a Naga freedom fighter, played a pivotal role in the fight against British colonial rule. Bir Tikendrajit Singh led the Manipur army against the British Empire. Kanaklata Barua from Assam, was a prominent freedom fighter who sacrificed her life during the Quit India Movement.

In recognition of their immense contributions to the nation, the central government has elevated these icons to national status. This acknowledgement not only celebrates their bravery and sacrifices but also highlights the rich cultural tapestry of Northeast India.

The Northeast is known for its vibrant festivals that showcase its diverse cultural heritage. Two prominent festivals, the Hornbill Festival in Nagaland and the Sangai Festival in Manipur, have gained popularity across the country. The Hornbill Festival, held annually in Nagaland, is a 10-day extravaganza that attracts visitors from all parts of the country. It showcases the vibrant traditions, art, music and dance forms of the Naga tribes. Prime Minister Modi created history by becoming the first-ever PM to inaugurate this tribal festival in Nagaland.

Similarly, the Sangai Festival of Manipur celebrates its rich cultural heritage. It highlights the indigenous dance forms, traditional sports, handicrafts and culinary delights of Manipur. These festivals not only promote tourism in the region but also provide a platform for cultural exchange and strengthen national integration.

Global Growth

Fertile lands and rich biodiversity are important assets of the Northeast. In recent years, the central government has taken several initiatives to promote natural farming practices in the region. One such initiative is the Krishi UDAN scheme, which enables farmers to send their agricultural products to various parts of the country.

As a result of these efforts, the region has witnessed an impressive 85 per cent growth in the export of agricultural products over the past six years.[1] The promotion of natural farming practices not only ensures sustainable agricultural

---

[1]Anand, Saurav, 'Northeast India Sees over 85% Agricultural Product Export Growth in Last 6 Years', *Livemint*, 2 December 2022, https://tinyurl.com/3rwvakzn. Accessed on 12 September 2023.

practices but also provides economic opportunities to the farmers of the Northeast.

Significant strides have been made in the realm of infrastructure development in the Northeast over the past few years. The number of airports has increased from nine to 16 within the last nine years, bolstering air connectivity and giving a substantial boost to tourism and trade. Moreover, after a staggering 75-year wait, Manipur and Meghalaya have finally been connected by the first-ever goods train in 2022 and 2023, respectively. Additionally, the length of national highways in the region has surged by 50 per cent since 2014, leading to better road connectivity and fostering economic growth. The government's dedicated investment of over ₹95,000 crore in 21 railway projects, aimed at connecting Manipur, Mizoram and Meghalaya by the end of 2023, and the capital of Nagaland by 2026, is yet another milestone in enhancing rail connectivity, accessibility and overall development in the region.

Furthermore, the government has been unwavering in its focus on infrastructure development, with 4,016 km of road projects currently underway. The completion of the Bogibeel Bridge, after a 16-year delay, stands as a testament to the commitment to overcome challenges and fulfil the aspirations of the people. Prime Minister Narendra Modi's remarkable dedication to the Northeast is evident in his record-breaking 60 visits to the region since 2014, the highest number of visits by any PM till date. These visits underscore his vision for inclusive growth and development, firmly believing in the Northeast's potential as an integral part of India's growth narrative.

Under PM Modi's leadership, several initiatives have been undertaken to promote tourism, improve education and medical infrastructure and provide skill-based training to women. The establishment of the first All India Institute of Medical Sciences (AIIMS) in the Northeast at Guwahati is a major milestone in the region's healthcare journey. This world-class medical institution will not only provide quality healthcare to the people of Assam but will also benefit other Northeastern states. The Pradhan Mantri Kaushal Vikas Yojana (PMKVY) has been instrumental in providing skill training to women in sectors such as information technology (IT), hospitality and manufacturing. This initiative has helped to empower women and create new opportunities for them in the workforce.

Towards Peace and Prosperity

The Northeast region has grappled with the complex issue of the Armed Forces (Special Powers) Act (AFSPA) for a considerable period of time. However, commendable progress has been achieved in reducing the areas under the AFSPA in recent years. Notably, insurgency in the region has witnessed a significant decline of 76 per cent in 2022 from 2014, creating an environment of peace and progress. Various peace accords with different insurgent groups have further bolstered the government's efforts to establish lasting peace. These include the historic Framework Agreement (FA) with the National Socialist Council of Nagalim–Issak and Muivah (NSCN-IM) in 2015, the Tripura Peace Accord with the National Liberation Front of Twipra led by Sabir Kumar Debbarma (NLFT-SD) in 2019, the Bodo Peace Accord in 2020, the Bru Rehabilitation Agreement in 2020, the Karbi-Anglong Peace Accord in 2021, the Assam-Meghalaya boundary agreement in 2022 and the Assam Adivasi Peace Accord in 2022. The successful implementation of these accords has led to a substantial reduction in insurgency and civilian casualties in the region.

The increased representation of the Northeast in PM Modi's Cabinet, the recognition of national icons, the promotion of cultural festivals, the focus on natural farming and infrastructure development, the reduction of AFSPA and the successful peace accords have collectively transformed the Northeast region of India. Prime Minister Modi's vision and dedicated efforts have brought about remarkable positive changes, fostering connectivity, driving economic growth and ensuring a peaceful and inclusive future for the region. These initiatives reflect the resolute commitment of the government to development and progress of the Northeast, further cementing its rightful place in India's growth story.

7

FROM NEGLECT TO DEVELOPMENT: POLICIES AND PROGRESS

Tejasvi Surya

The visionary approach adopted by the National Democratic Alliance (NDA) government led by the Bharatiya Janata Party (BJP) has ushered in an era of remarkable advancement and prosperity, firmly establishing the Northeast as a beacon of hope and growth. With a strong focus on peace, progress and prosperity, the government has spearheaded unprecedented development across the nation.

Under the previous administration at the Centre, the Northeast region was largely excluded from the overall development plans and initiatives. During that period, the region was frequently in the spotlight for incidents of terrorism, civil unrest and blockades, leading to the tragic loss of innocent lives. Sadly, the promise of development remained distant and confined mainly to official documents. Since the formation of the government led by Prime Minister (PM) Narendra Modi in 2014, the Northeast region of India has witnessed a remarkable transformation. Historically known for its geographical isolation, neglect and insurgency issues, the region has emerged as a hub of progress and development in recent times. This chapter explores the significant efforts and policies implemented by the Modi government that have facilitated the socio-economic growth, improved connectivity in the Northeast and bolstered its position on the national and international stage.

Prime Minister Modi's 60 unprecedented visits to the Northeast not only set a remarkable record for any PM but also serve as a testament to his prioritization of the region. Through his repeated presence in the region, the entire government machinery comprehends and acknowledges the immense importance and value of the Northeast region.

In order to significantly increase the allocation of resources to the Northeast and address the existing gaps in basic services and infrastructure, central ministries and departments are required to allocate 10 per cent of their gross budgetary support (GBS) for the development of the region. Unless specifically exempted, this provision applies to both central sector (CS) schemes and centrally sponsored schemes (CSS). According to available budget data from 2014–15 to 2020–21, non-exempted central government ministries and departments have spent a total of ₹265,766.67 crore in the Northeastern region.[1]

The unwavering determination to uplift the region is epitomized by the staggering expenditure over the course of the past nine years, surpassing the cumulative spending of the preceding 25 years. This unprecedented financial support stands as a testament to the unwavering dedication of the government, playing a pivotal role in fostering the region's growth and effectively bridging the developmental divide.

Revitalizing the Economy

Following the assumption of power by PM Atal Bihari Vajpayee's administration, the Northeastern region underwent notable transformations. He was the first PM to spend a night in the Northeast. Under PM Vajpayee, genuine efforts were made to alter the narrative of decades of neglect, exemplified by the establishment of a dedicated ministry for the development of the

---

[1] 'Budget Series #10: Prime Minister's Development Initiative for North East (PM-DevINE)', *pib.gov*, 3 March 2022, https://tinyurl.com/abazjdsu. Accessed on 13 September 2023.

Northeast. Regrettably, subsequent governments failed to sustain the momentum until the arrival of the Modi government. Unlike previous administrations that regarded the Northeast as a distant entity, the Modi government held the steadfast belief that the villages situated in border areas were not the last but rather the first villages of our nation.

Prime Minister Modi announced a new central scheme in the Budget 2022–23, which obtained Cabinet approval on 12 October 2022. It was known as the Prime Minister's Development Initiative for the North East Region (PM-DevINE), a scheme aiming to promote the idea and objective of PM Gati Shakti by providing the necessary funds for infrastructure development alongside supporting projects for social development. The PM-DevINE scheme not only promulgates livelihood activities for youth and women but also fills the lacunae in development in various sectors across the Northeastern states. This scheme is fully funded by the central government, and it outlays an expenditure of ₹6,600 crores during the period from 2022–23 to 2025–26.[2]

The Modi government has progressed from the 'Look East' policy to a more proactive 'Act East' approach, and today, it has moved to 'Act Fast for Northeast' and 'Act First for Northeast', as PM Modi highlighted in his speech from December 2022.[3] Over the past nine years, his intensified focus has resulted in accelerated development and priority attention to the region. Over the years, strategic infrastructure projects, improved connectivity and targeted initiatives have paved the way for enhanced economic growth, employment opportunities and overall progress in the Northeast. The government's unwavering commitment to the region has brought about a new era of prosperity and inclusivity.

---

[2]'Prime Minister's Development Initiative for North Eastern Region (PM-DevINE)-Issue of Revised Guidelines', *PIBDelhi*, 21 August 2023, https://tinyurl.com/37avet7t. Accessed on 13 September 2023.

[3]'PM Addresses Meeting of North Eastern Council in Shillong', *PIBDelhi*, 18 December 2022, https://tinyurl.com/4sdkfaz7. Accessed on 13 September 2023.

The government's 'Act East' policy has been focusing on addressing infrastructural, logistical and connectivity challenges through targeted plans. One such initiative, the Mission Organic Value Chain Development for North Eastern Region (MOVCDNER) 2017, aimed to connect farmers in the region with potential customers and provide support in accessing organic inputs, thereby addressing infrastructural gaps. Furthermore, efforts have been made to establish an enhanced and connected transport network, such as the Trans-Asian Railway network. This network can serve as a gateway to the Association of Southeast Asian Nations (ASEAN) countries, which is beneficial, as the ASEAN economy recognizes India's voluntary certifications under the Participatory Guarantee System of India (PGS-India) scheme. Additionally, the One District One Product (ODOP) initiative can play a significant role in boosting the region's economic performance. By encouraging individual districts to focus on specific niche products, this initiative can provide institutional support for logistics, storage, connectivity and networking with foreign buyers, which are crucial for the region's growth.[4]

Infrastructure and Development

Northeast India has witnessed significant developments in terms of transportation infrastructure. The increase in the number of airports from nine to 16 indicates a positive trend in improving air connectivity in the region. The rise in the number of flights from around 900 before 2014 to approximately 1,900 showcases an increased frequency of air travel, which can greatly benefit the people residing in the Northeast.[5]

---

[4]Deb, Srijata, 'Tapping into the Potential of Northeast India's Organic Produce', *Trade Promotion Council of India*, 21 February 2022, https://tinyurl.com/dbyzw6tt. Accessed on 13 September 2023.

[5]'PM Addresses Meeting of North Eastern Council in Shillong', *PIBDelhi*, 18 December 2022, https://tinyurl.com/4sdkfaz7. Accessed on 13 September 2023.

The inclusion of the Northeastern states on India's railway map for the first time is a noteworthy achievement. Expanding the railway network in the region allows better connectivity with other parts of the country, thereby facilitating the movement of people and goods. This development can contribute to the overall economic growth and development of the Northeastern states. Efforts to expand waterways in the Northeast are also promising. Enhancing the region's water transport infrastructure can provide an alternative mode of transportation, particularly for cargo movement. This expansion can leverage the region's rivers and water bodies, promoting trade and commerce while reducing the strain on road and air transportation.

The ongoing infrastructure projects aimed at enhancing road connectivity in the Northeastern region include significant initiatives such as the construction of an alternative two-lane highway spanning 152 km from Bagrakote to Pakyong (NH 717A) in Sikkim. Additionally, efforts are underway to expand the Imphal-Moreh section of NH 39 over a distance of 20 km, as well as to improve the existing two-lane stretch of 75.4 km in Manipur. Furthermore, the government is focussed on four-laning the Dimapur–Kohima road, covering a distance of 62.9 km in Nagaland. Another important project involves the four-laning of the Nagaon bypass to Holongi, spanning 167 km in Arunachal Pradesh. Moreover, the two-laning of the Aizawl–Tuipang NH 54, extending over 351 km in Mizoram, is also being undertaken.[6]

In addition to the efforts to enhance physical connectivity, the government is actively working on improving digital connectivity in the Northeastern region. This endeavour involves expanding the optical fibre network, which will contribute to the development and growth of various sectors, including the start-up ecosystem

---

[6]'In Last 03 Years Total 4686 km National Highways Sanctioned Rs 60,093 Crore by the Ministry of Road Transport and Highways in the North Eastern Region', *PIBDelhi*, 27 March 2023, https://tinyurl.com/murdrwta. Accessed on 13 September 2023.

and the service sector. The implementation of 5G technology is expected to play a crucial role in furthering the advancement of these sectors and promoting overall economic progress in the region.

The Bogibeel Bridge is a combined rail and road bridge over the Brahmaputra River in the Northeastern state of Assam. It connects the districts of Dibrugarh and Dhemaji, and it is the longest rail-cum-road bridge in India. However, due to various reasons, such as environmental concerns, land acquisition issues and financial constraints, the construction of the bridge faced delays. It was under the leadership of PM Modi that the project gained momentum and was finally completed. The Bogibeel Bridge was inaugurated by PM Modi on 25 December 2018. The completion of the bridge was indeed a significant milestone for the region, as it provided a vital link for transportation and connectivity in the Northeastern part of India. The completion of the Bogibeel Bridge demonstrates the commitment of the government to develop and improve connectivity in the region.

In addition to the peace agreements, the central government has focussed on improving connectivity in the Northeast. It includes the ambitious goal of connecting all parts of the region to India's railway network. Notably, three state capitals—Assam, Tripura and Arunachal Pradesh—are already connected by broad gauge rail, and efforts are underway to connect other state capitals. This improved connectivity has the potential to bring about significant economic opportunities and growth for the region. By reducing travel time between the Northeast and other states, it facilitates the movement of goods and enables the sale of products from the Northeast throughout the country. Enhanced economic activity will help reduce migration for employment and contribute to the overall development of the region.

Overall, these initiatives indicate a concerted effort to improve connectivity and transportation infrastructure in Northeast India. By enhancing air, rail and waterway networks, the region can experience increased economic activity, tourism and improved accessibility for its residents.

Establishing Peace

Due to the consistent efforts of the government, several peace agreements have been signed with various insurgent groups, resulting in a substantial reduction in violence and insurgency. Significant progress has been made in terms of peace and development in recent years. These agreements include the Framework Agreement with the National Socialist Council of Nagaland-Isak-Muivah (NSCN-IM) in 2015, the Tripura Peace Accord in 2019 involving the National Liberation Front of Tripura (NLFT/SD), the Bodo Peace Accord in 2020, the Bru Rehabilitation Agreement in 2020, the Karbi-Anglong Peace Accord in 2021, the Assam-Meghalaya boundary agreement in 2022 and the Assam Adivasi Peace Accord in 2022. Through these, long-standing border disputes have been resolved and a sense of stability and security has been brought to the region.

As peace is returning due to the collective efforts of the government and society, the old laws are also being reformed. Between 2006 and 2014, the country witnessed 8,700 incidents of violence in the Northeast, which came down by 74 per cent under the Modi government.[7] During the last eight years, the Modi government has removed the Armed Forces (Special Powers) Act (AFSPA) from many areas of the Northeast to ensure permanent peace and better law and order situation. The areas under AFSPA in the Northeast have been reduced significantly. The AFSPA has been removed from 23 districts of Assam. In 2015 and 2018, the AFSPA was fully withdrawn from Tripura and Meghalaya, respectively. There are ongoing efforts to repeal the AFSPA in more areas as well. In other states like Nagaland, too, we are

---

[7]@BJP4India, *X* (formerly *Twitter*), 14 February 2023, 4.46 p.m., https://tinyurl.com/45xnht2d. Accessed on 13 September 2023.

rapidly progressing in this direction. Today, AFSPA is partially applicable in only 12 districts of the Northeast. Data from the Union Home Ministry reveals that insurgency-related incidents in the Northeastern states dipped by 80 per cent and civilian deaths by 99 per cent last year compared to 2014. The civilian deaths were in single digits (two) in 2020 for the first time since 1999. The deaths of security forces personnel also came down by 75 per cent.[8] There were around 1,963 incidents in 2000 where 811 people were kidnapped, 1,536 extremists were arrested and 585 extremists were killed. In contrast, as per the 2022 security data (which is the latest data), there were around 201 incidents, 103 kidnappings, 563 extremist arrests and six extremist kills.[9]

From the Hills to the Olympics

The Northeast has been producing some of the most acclaimed international athletes and sportspersons. The most notable among them is Mary Kom, who hails from Manipur and is a six-time world boxing champion and an Olympic bronze medallist. Another regional Olympic medallist is Dipa Karmakar, a gymnast from Tripura and the first Indian female gymnast to compete in the Olympics. The Modi government has undertaken several initiatives to boost the sporting potential of the Northeastern states, including setting up state-of-the-art sports facilities, establishing sports academies and organizing various tournaments. Netaji Subhas Regional Coaching Centre (NSRCC) Sports Complex, NIT and other state-of-the-art indoor sports complex have been built in Agartala and Tripura, featuring a gymnastics hall, shooting range, indoor stadium, and many more.

---

[8]Chauhan, Neeraj, 'Insurgency-Related Incidents Dipped by 80% In N-E States Last Year: MHA Data', *Hindustan Times*, 2 March 2021, https://tinyurl.com/45sd54by. Accessed on 13 September 2023.

[9]'Insurgency in North East', *Ministry of Home Affairs*, March 2023, https://tinyurl.com/2jc2mdmh. Accessed on 24 September 2023.

The Northeast today is benefiting from focussed schemes and efforts like the Target Olympic Podium Scheme (TOPS), ensuring that a 'core group of athletes' have all the necessary personalized support in terms of foreign exposure, hiring of specific coaches, training and competition abroad or 'Khelo India', promoting local sports and nurturing talents.[10]

The visionary approach adopted by the NDA government led by the BJP has ushered in a new era of progress and prosperity for the Northeast region of India. Through unprecedented financial support, focussed policies and unwavering commitment, the Modi government has successfully transformed a historically underdeveloped and isolated region into a symbol of hope and growth. Significant efforts have been made to bridge the developmental divide, enhance connectivity and promote economic opportunities. The establishment of dedicated ministries, infrastructure projects and peace agreements has played a crucial role in fostering socio-economic growth and stability. The future has never looked so bright for the youth and future generations.

It is a testament to the resilience of its people and the transformative vision of our government. Together, we have built bridges of progress, connecting hearts, minds and dreams. Let the Northeast's story inspire us all to reach the highest peaks and overcome the deepest valleys, for when we invest in the growth of every region, we unlock the true potential of our nation.

---

[10]Sindhu, PV, 'India Bid under Modi to Become Sports Superpower', *The New Indian Express*, 17 September 2022, https://tinyurl.com/mphnmfwj. Accessed on 24 September 2023.

8

THE NORTHEAST: A PERSONAL JOURNEY

Vivek Singh and Rouhin Deb

The journey of the Northeast during the tenure of Prime Minister (PM) Narendra Modi has been nothing short of a personal experience for us. It's like witnessing a dear friend undergo a beautiful transformation, becoming an integral part of India's growth story. The government didn't just address the needs and concerns of the region; it did so while embracing the region's rich culture, languages and traditions. It's as if they connected the Northeast with the rest of India and also linked it to the global stage.

When Narendra Modi became the PM of India in 2014, he had a vision of transforming India. He put the Northeast at the heart of his vision. He changed the 'Look East Policy' to 'Act East Policy' and took a holistic approach to tackle the challenges of the region. He asked all Union Ministers to visit the region and spend a night there every two months to ensure better integration of the region with the national policies and programmes.[1] Since then, on his nearly 60 visits to the Northeast, he has inaugurated many projects, held rallies and roadshows, and attended swearing-in ceremonies

[1]'PM Narendra Modi Makes One-Night Stays Mandatory for Ministers Visiting Northeast', *Financial Express*, 19 May 2017, https://tinyurl.com/5yhhvsns. Accessed on 13 September 2023.

of North-East Democratic Alliance (NEDA) governments. He has followed his vision of 'Sabka Saath, Sabka Vikas', and pushed for the development of infrastructure to reduce the distance between Delhi and the Northeast both literally and figuratively, as well as the promotion of social harmony and upliftment of the people through welfare schemes, healthcare, education, etc.

The Northeast has undergone a tremendous economic transformation under the Modi government. The cumulative gross domestic product (GDP) of the Northeastern states has more than doubled from 2.97 lakh crore to 6.81 lakh crore, and their share of the Indian GDP has increased from 2.6 per cent in 2013–14 to 2.9 per cent in 2021–22[2]. This is largely due to the massive improvement in the region's connectivity, which has opened up new avenues of economic opportunity for the people. The government has invested in highway projects, bridges, railway lines, airports and the development of waterways. These upgraded infrastructures have also helped in delivering public goods to the remotest corners of the region. Assam in particular has witnessed unprecedented development in recent times, with the addition of several new bridges, expansion of roads and highways, and ongoing construction of a tunnel under the Brahmaputra. This infrastructural boost has fostered economic growth through enhanced connectivity via road, air and sea. Similar sweeping changes have also benefited the healthcare and education sectors, leaving no one behind. The Northeast has achieved a newfound relevance, one that fills us with pride.

From Isolation to Involvement

The Northeast is a region of incredible diversity and beauty, but it is also a region of pain and struggle. For too long, the people

---

[2]Dhasmana, Indivjal, 'In Contrast to UPA Years, NER's Economy Has Seen Gradual Growth in NDA Rule', *Business Standard,* 13 August 2024, https://tinyurl.com/ymvkz67m. Accessed on 8 December 2023.

of the region, belonging to nearly 200 distinct and unique tribal communities, have been treated as 'lesser Indians' and neglected by the Indian state. Some of them resorted to violence and insurgencies, demanding autonomy or secession. The region was engulfed in bloodshed, chaos and fear. The region also faced border disputes among the states, which often led to clashes and tension.

This grim scenario changed when the Bharatiya Janata Party (BJP) government came to power in 2014 and took landmark steps to promote social harmony and peace in the region. The government has shown respect and sensitivity towards the culture, identity and dignity of the people of the region and has engaged in dialogue, development and democracy to address the grievances and aspirations of the people. The government has made efforts for the surrender of militants through various peace talks and accords, the rehabilitation of surrendered insurgents, the creation of several autonomous councils for different tribal groups, the removal of the Armed Forces (Special Powers) Act (AFSPA) from several districts, and the reduction of border conflicts, among many other measures. The signing of the Karbi Peace Accord, the Assam Adivasi Peace Accord, Dimasa Peace Accord and the Bodo Peace Accord are examples of how the government has made a lasting difference.

The Modi government has also resolved the long-standing border disputes among the states in the region with a unique policy, aided by Union Home Minister Amit Shah. All states formed five-member regional committees headed by a State Cabinet Minister, including bureaucrats and local representatives. These bodies visited each and every disputed area, analysed the exchange of land records, conducted detailed deliberations and negotiations and sent the final recommendations to their respective state governments, upon which various Chief Minister-level and Cabinet-level talks and negotiations were held to clearly demarcate the disputed sites so as to reflect the will of the people.

Digitizing and Protecting Industry

Prime Minister Modi's commitment to the development of the Northeast and the financial empowerment of its people has enabled them to access formal financial services at an affordable cost, which is crucial for creating jobs, boosting growth, eradicating poverty and fostering social harmony. The JAM Trinity (Jan Dhan, Aadhar and Mobile) is a game-changer in the financial inclusion scenario of the Northeast. The people of the region who were once deprived of banking facilities are now enjoying benefits such as bank accounts with RuPay cards that allow them to make digital transactions; direct benefit transfers that ensure timely delivery of subsidies; insurance schemes that provide security; pension schemes that provide dignity; and Mudra loans that provide opportunity. These innovative and effective measures have also been aptly complemented by the BJP-led state governments in the region. For example, the Assam government introduced the Orunodoi scheme. The sum disbursed through this scheme, along with other pensions given to widows, *divyangs*, etc., reaches the beneficiaries on time because of the availability of Jan Dhan bank accounts. This banking revolution has been a truly remarkable boon for public service delivery in the Northeast.

The Modi government has also taken special care of the tea garden workers and their families in Assam and West Bengal, who are an integral part of the region's economy and culture. The government announced an unprecedented ₹1,000 crore in the Union Budget 2020–21 for the welfare of women tea garden workers and their children in terms of health, education, skill development, etc.[3] The government has also introduced several measures to improve the quality and productivity of the tea industry in India, such as setting up a fully transparent e-auction platform for tea, which has resulted in a 40 per cent increase in the green

[3]'Union Budget 2021: Govt Proposes Rs 1,000 Crore for Welfare of Tea Workers in Assam, West Bengal', *India Today*, 1 February 2021, https://tinyurl.com/3z37unnz. Accessed on 13 September 2023.

leaf price. This is benefiting the small plantation farmers and protecting the intellectual property of Darjeeling tea and Assam tea in about 40 countries. This is safeguarding the brand and fetching remunerative prices, leading to job creation—providing around ₹63 crore[4] as a subsidy to the tea industry across India and giving special focus to the labourers during the Covid-19 pandemic. Furthermore, this is easing the compliance burden of the tea gardens by increasing the threshold of paid-up capital and turnover for small companies and subsuming the Plantation Labour Act in the new Labour Codes, which provide multiple benefits like sickness benefits, unemployment allowance, maternity benefits, etc., to the workers. We have seen how this push by the Centre has empowered state governments such as Assam to complement the policies and improve public service delivery in areas with tea gardens.

Apart from significantly raising the daily wage, the government has built several schools and hospitals, placed telecom towers in remote gardens, provided mobile phones to Line Sardars, and constructed ATMs and banking facilities, resulting in the holistic development of these tea garden areas.

Spotlight on Progress

We were lucky enough to witness this cultural metamorphosis ourselves when we studied at IIM (Indian Institutes of Management) Shillong, where we spent two years between 2014 and 2016 during PM Modi's tenure and saw how the region was changing rapidly in various fields such as peace, infrastructure, social welfare, education, health, skill development, etc. The Northeast also got its first-ever All India Institute of Medical Sciences (AIIMS) in the 75th year of Independence at Guwahati. Other landmark measures, such as the expansion of internet

---

[4]'Assam Tea Gardens Get Rs 63 Crore Govt Assistance To Tackle Pandemic Losses', *Outlook*, 31 March 2023, https://tinyurl.com/2p8xvatd. Accessed on 24 September 2023.

technology to the Northeast, have augmented education by enabling e-learning for students through smart classrooms, thereby digitizing education for the twenty-first century.

We remember how PM Modi inaugurated a new railway line connecting Meghalaya with Assam in 2014, which was a historic moment for the people of both states. We also remember how PM Modi launched a new scheme called Pradhan Mantri Ujjwala Yojana (PMUY) in 2016, which provided free liquefied petroleum gas (LPG) connections to poor women in rural areas, thereby improving their health and living standards. Later, we also got a chance to work in the finance ministry and with the Government of Assam respectively, and saw how PM Modi personally monitored and reviewed the progress and impact of various initiatives taken for the development and integration of the Northeast. We have observed how the Northeast has become a priority and pride for the PM and his team and have witnessed how the Northeast has become a model and an inspiration for the rest of India. We have realized how the Northeast has become a new paradigm that is transforming India.

In 2022, when PM Modi launched the Har Ghar Tiranga movement to mark Azadi Ka Amrit Mahotsav, it was no surprise that the people of the Northeast actively participated. Unlike the turbulent decades of the 1960s to 1990s, when raising the national flag would have invited the ire of militants, a spirit of nationalism now fills the hearts of the people of the region. Even the national anthem was played in the Nagaland Legislative Assembly for the first time. In a sense, integration of the Northeast is finally complete after 75 years of Indian independence.

To conclude, in India's grand tapestry, the Northeast has emerged as a pivotal thread, not confined to the periphery but intricately woven into the fabric of national progress. This metamorphosis, witnessed through our own experiences, is a testament to the Modi government's vision and its unwavering dedication to shaping a united and vibrant India.

9

UNLEASHING THE POWER OF THE NORTHEAST

Raju Bista

For far too long, the Northeast region has been plagued by geographical isolation and neglect from the central government. Growing up in the remote village of Charhajare in Manipur during the turbulent 80s and 90s, I witnessed first-hand the challenges posed by insurgency, violence and political unrest. The then-government was conspicuous by their absence, and the majority of the people felt abandoned by the negligence of the government. There was no ray of hope for the common citizens; infrastructure was non-existent, unemployment was rife and the entire region was engulfed in strife of one form or another. There was no future for the youth in the region, which caused thousands of youngsters to migrate to bigger cities outside of the Northeast. The dream of development seemed far-fetched. Opportunities for the youth to showcase their potential were scarce.

After a long wait, the tide had turned for the eight Northeastern states of India, thanks to the leadership intervention of Prime Minister (PM) Narendra Modi. Since assuming office in 2014, PM Modi has prioritized the development of the Northeastern states. With his visionary approach encapsulated in the 'Act East' policies, PM Modi has ushered in a transformative era aimed at unleashing the region's true potential. With a rich history, diverse cultural heritage and immense potential, the Northeastern states are now on the path to becoming the next frontier of growth for India.

Funding Development

A key aspect of PM Modi's vision for the Northeast is the focus on infrastructure development. Recognizing the need to bridge the connectivity gap, the government has embarked on ambitious projects in the region. From improving air, rail and road connectivity to harnessing the power of telecommunications and waterways, significant strides have been made to integrate the Northeast with the rest of the country.

Under the Modi government, an unprecedented focus has been placed on allocating financial resources to the region. The yearly budget allocation for the development of the Northeastern states has increased by over 265 per cent since 2014–15, reaching ₹76,540.28 crore in 2022–23. This remarkable surge in funding, totalling over ₹384,561.62 crores in the past nine years, has been instrumental in boosting the regional economy and connectivity.

With greater funding, there has been a transformation in the infrastructure of the region. Improvement in infrastructure helps in lowering the cost of production, thus enhancing the level of output produced for a given cost. Infrastructure development causes the markets to work better in favour of a region. By recognizing the pressing need for enhanced infrastructure in the Northeast, the central government has undertaken a comprehensive developmental strategy to foster projects that rapidly bring the region at par with the rest of the country and enhance economic opportunities for the people in the region.

Road Infrastructure

As part of the Act East Policy, the government has successfully completed major highway development projects, resulting in the construction of 3099.50 km of roads in the region. Ongoing projects aim to connect an additional 4,016.22 km, significantly improving regional and national connectivity.[1] Notable ongoing projects include the four-laning of Dimapur–Kohima Road (62.9 km) in Nagaland, the four-laning of Nagaon bypass to Holongi (167 km) in Arunachal Pradesh, the the two-laning of Aizawl-Tuipang NH 54 (351 km) in Mizoram, the construction of Shillong-Dawki road (44 km) and seven highway projects worth over ₹10,000 crore have been announced for Tripura. In the last seven years, the Ministry of Road Transport and Highways (MoRTH) has completed 4,121 km of road projects in the Northeast, with 7,545 km of ongoing projects totalling ₹105,518 crore.[2]

Rail Infrastructure

To ensure the integration of all Northeastern states with the national rail grid, the government has sanctioned new projects spanning 864.7 km and amounting to ₹19,855 crores. Presently, 20 projects for new lines and doubling, costing ₹74,485 crore for a length of 2,011 km in the Northeastern region, are at different stages of planning, approval and execution. Out of these, 321 km have been commissioned with an expenditure of ₹26,874 crore, facilitating greater accessibility and integration. The Sivok–Rangpo rail line will connect Sikkim and the important China border with the national rail grid. In Manipur, 93 per cent of physical work has been completed on the important Jiribam–Imphal railway line.[3]

---

[1] 'Infrastructure Developement in North Eastern States', *PIBDelhi*, 10 February 2024, https://tinyurl.com/5xrz8zvk. Accessed on 8 December 2023.

[2] 'Rs.3.84 Lakh Crore Spent by 55 Non-exempted Central Ministries/ Departments under 10% GBS for the Development of Infrastructure in the North Eastern States since 2014-15', *PIBDelhi*, 13 March 2023, https://tinyurl.com/2axzc84w. Accessed on 24 September 2023.

[3] 'Jiribam-Imphal New Line Railway Project in Manipur Achieved 93 per Cent Progress', *ANI*, 2 April 2023, https://tinyurl.com/6r8jvmp9. Accessed on 8 December 2023.

Air Infrastructure

The government has prioritized the development of aviation infrastructure and improved air connectivity in the Northeast through the 'Ude Desh ka Aam Naagrik' (UDAN) scheme. With 29 completed air connectivity projects, the region has witnessed a significant upswing in regional connectivity and tourism. Recent developments include the inauguration of Donyi Polo Airport (formerly Holongi Airport) in Arunachal Pradesh, the redevelopment of Maharaja Bir Bikram Airport in Agartala, Tripura and the construction of new Greenfield Airports in Arunachal Pradesh and Barapani Airport in Meghalaya.

Telecom Infrastructure

Addressing the long-standing issue of inadequate telecom connectivity, the Department of Telecommunications has undertaken projects to strengthen telecom infrastructure in the Northeastern states. With 1,358 installed towers providing services across 1,246 villages, significant progress has been made in overcoming communication barriers.[4]

Unlocking the Economic Potential

The Northeastern states boast of abundant human capital, natural resources and breathtaking landscapes. Given its strategic location as the gateway to Southeast Asia, the region is an exciting destination for international trade and commerce. Under the leadership of PM Modi, there has been a renewed focus on unlocking this potential, resulting in increased investment and job opportunities in the region. As a result, sectors like tourism,

---

[4] 'Rs.3.84 Lakh Crore Spent by 55 Non-exempted Central Ministries/ Departments under 10% GBS for the Development of Infrastructure in the North Eastern States since 2014-15', *PIBDelhi*, 13 March 2023, https://tinyurl.com/2axzc84w. Accessed on 24 September 2023.

agriculture and international trade are being propelled towards significant growth and sustainable development, ultimately leading to prosperity.

The tourism industry in the Northeastern states has witnessed significant growth as a result of improved infrastructure and connectivity. The region's awe-inspiring landscapes, pristine forests and diverse cultural heritage have become major attractions for travellers. The region registered a record-breaking tourist footfall of one lakh foreign guests and over 11.8 million domestic visitors during the last one year.[5] The surge in tourist footfall has not only boosted the hospitality sector but also created opportunities for local artisans, handicraft makers and cultural entrepreneurs to showcase their unique offerings. This, in turn, stimulates economic growth at the grassroots and fosters cultural exchange.

Agriculture, another crucial sector in the Northeast, has experienced a remarkable transformation. The implementation of advanced farming techniques and the adoption of scientific practices have enhanced productivity and quality. Additionally, the government's focus on promoting organic farming has positioned the region as a hub for organic produce, catering to the growing demand for healthy and sustainable food products. Some special crops with significant market demand are grown in the North Eastern Region (NER), including Assam lemon, Joha rice, medicinal rice and passion fruits. The NER is responsible for 45 per cent of India's total pineapple output and is the fourth-largest orange grower. Sikkim produces the majority of the world's large cardamom, approximately 54 per cent of it.[6] This has not only provided farmers with better livelihood opportunities but has also contributed to the overall economic growth of the region.

---

[5]Kalita, Kangkan, 'PM Narendra Modi Hails Record Footfall of Tourists in Northeast region', *The Times of India*, 5 April 2023, https://tinyurl.com/2macz8cm. Accessed on 24 September 2023.

[6]Kandwal, Shruti, 'Organic Farming in North East India: Key Facts', *Krishi Jagran*, 17 January 2023, https://tinyurl.com/2exu5ck5. Accessed on 24 September 2023.

Empowering Youth

The central government has placed special emphasis on empowering the youth of the region and acknowledging their immense talent and potential. In order to harness their capabilities and contribute to their holistic development, a range of initiatives have been introduced, including skill development programmes, educational opportunities and platforms for showcasing their abilities. These efforts are aimed at fostering a vibrant and dynamic generation that will serve as the driving force behind the region's future growth and progress.

Through these initiatives, the government is not only investing in the future of the region but also fostering a sense of pride, purpose and inclusivity among the young population, creating a dynamic generation that will drive the region's growth along with the nation's, contributing to holistic progress and pride, and serving as a source of inspiration for generations to come.

As a result of these multifaceted efforts, the Northeast region is breaking free from the shadows of neglect and isolation. Under the dedicated leadership of PM Modi, the region is experiencing a renaissance of development and progress. With a focus on supporting the local economy at its core, coupled with improved connectivity, investment in infrastructure and economic empowerment, the Northeast is poised to realize its full potential as a vibrant and prosperous region.

10

GATEWAY TO SOUTHEAST ASIA

Vaibhav Dange

The Northeast has always been considered India's gateway to Southeast Asia. The road to growth and prosperity of Northeast India opens up only with greater cultural, economic and commercial interactions with our neighbours in the East and the Association of Southeast Asian Nations (ASEAN). The eight states of the Northeast—Assam, Arunachal Pradesh, Manipur, Meghalaya, Mizoram, Nagaland, Sikkim and Tripura, not only share their borders with their neighbouring countries—Bhutan, China, Myanmar and Bangladesh—but also share social and cultural connections. There have been centuries-old trade relations between the Northeastern states of India and South Asia, which has been referred to as 'Suvarnabhumi' (land of gold) in ancient texts. After 2014, a major impetus was given to further strengthen this relationship between the Indian Northeast and the Southeast Asia.

The biggest bottleneck in the development of the Northeast has been the connectivity within India domestically and with neighbours internationally. The geographical and climatic difficulties in Northeast India makes the problem even more complex. Improving connectivity and providing better infrastructure, be it road, rail, air or through waterways takes long and requires a very high public investment. After 2014, a major paradigm shift came up and suddenly, the Northeast was buzzing with new large scale infrastructure projects, particularly in the roadways.

Prime Minister (PM) Narendra Modi envisioned 'Transformation by Transportation', which has been taken forward by the able leadership of Union Minister Nitin Gadkari. More than 3,800 km of National Highways projects worth ₹30,000 crore have been under various stages of development, under Bharatmala Pariyojana[1]. In addition, an investment of ₹60,000 crore under Special Accelerated Road Development[2] is already being implemented. Between 2014 and 2021, there has been 50 per cent increase in the length of national highways.[3] Majority of these are either completed or in their last leg of completion. The magnitude of highway development can be assessed by the fact that, till 2014 there were only two bridges on the mighty Brahmaputra River in Assam, whereas the last nine years have initiated more than six additional bridges with more than ₹9,000 crore of investment on Brahmaputra alone. The Dhola–Sadia Bridge, which is India's longest bridge built till today, is 9.5 km in length and has reduced the travel time between Assam and Arunachal Pradesh from 6–8 hours to less than 60 minutes; the distance has reduced from 165 km to 15 km.

---

[1]As defined on the official website, 'Bharatmala Pariyojana' is a new umbrella programme for the highways sector that focusses on optimizing efficiency of freight and passenger movement across the country by bridging critical infrastructure gaps through effective interventions like development of Economic Corridors, Inter Corridors and Feeder Routes, National Corridor Efficiency Improvement, Border and International connectivity roads, Coastal and Port connectivity roads and Green-field expressways; See more at: *India.gov.in*, https://tinyurl.com/arr8vzpn. Accessed on 8 December 2023.

[2]PTI, 'PM Modi Unveils Key Road, Power Projects to Boost Development in NE', *The Economic Times*, 16 December 2017, https://tinyurl.com/fmpk33z3. Accessed on 8 December 2023.

[3]PTI, 'National Highways Length Rises by 50 per Cent in 7 Years: Govt Sources', *The Economic Times*, 15 July 2022, https://tinyurl.com/2c28fx9x. Accessed on 8 December 2023.

ASEAN Transportation Agreements/BBIN Nexus

The initiative to promote international trade between the Northeastern states and South Asia was strengthened by improving the mechanism of Bangladesh, Bhutan, India and Nepal (BBIN) sub group. This group was earlier conceptualized as South Asian Association for Regional Cooperation (SAARC) member countries grouped for smooth and better transportation. However, our perennial offender, Pakistan, played spoilsport and there was no headway. I remember, during one such meeting in Thimphu, Bhutan, Nitin Gadkari proposed the BBIN grouping, ensuring Pakistan stays out of it. Under the BBIN agreement signed in 2015, the first bus service between Bangladesh and Nepal via India (Northeast and West Bengal) was flagged off by the Bangladesh PM and was received in India by the West Bengal Chief Minister and India's Minister for Road Transport and Highways.

Similarly, under an agreement between India and Bangladesh, movement of goods through water and road has been started between Kolkata and Agartala via Chattogram port of Bangladesh. Five additional ports have been added in addition to the existing six 'Ports of Call' under the Protocol on Inland Water Transit and Trade by both the countries.[4] The number of 'Indo-Bangladesh Protocol (IBP) routes' has been increased from eight to ten. The Northeast region is strategically positioned to provide access to the traditional domestic market of eastern India, as well as the proximity of the eastern states to neighbouring countries such as Bangladesh and Myanmar.

The ASEAN, the Bangladesh–China–India–Myanmar corridor, the ASEAN–India Free Trade Agreement[5], India,

---

[4]'Protocol on Inland Water Transit and Trade', *Ministry of External Affairs*, 6 June 2015, https://tinyurl.com/2s36kc48. Accessed on 14 September 2023.

[5]See more at: *ASEAN-India Free Trade Area (AIFTA)*, https://tinyurl.com/49t5h4sa. Accessed on 14 September 2023.

Myanmar and Thailand Motor Vehicle Agreement, Kaladan Multi-Modal Transit Transport Project are becoming a gateway to development rather than a tussle between Northeast India and South Asia. The importance of the Northeastern region has been enhanced with the South Asian Sub-Regional Economic Cooperation (SASEC) road connectivity programme, a move that will be significant, given China's ambitious One Belt One Road (OBOR) initiative.

Internal Initiatives and All-round Development

In the last nine years, concrete steps have been taken to connect the Northeast by air. The setting up of an aviation manpower training institute, the development of Rupsi Airport and the expansion of air connectivity to Dimapur have been ensured to connect the people of the region with the rest of India, as well as to promote tourism. The number of airports in the region have increased from nine to 16 and the number of flights has increased from 900 before 2014 to 1,900.

India's longest rail and road link, Bogibeel Bridge over the Brahmaputra River at Bogibeel, near the city of Dibrugarh in Assam, connects Assam and Arunachal Pradesh. This bridge is also of great importance from the strategic and security perspective. Rail expansion has not been done only in this area, but also the Dhansiri-Kohima railway track; Kohima has been connected with the Rajdhani Express, Tripura Sundari Express to the Northeast with the national railway network, which connects this region to other states of the country through railways. Work on the India–Myanmar–Thailand Trilateral Highway and the Agartala–Akhaura Rail Project is currently underway.

The Government of India (GoI) has showcased its commitment to the all-round development of the Northeastern region under the Act East Policy and to make it an economic hub connecting South East Asia. Prime Minister Narendra Modi himself has led this from the front by visiting Northeast for more than 60 times in the last nine years. The total earmarked funds under 10 per cent Gross Budgetary Support from 54 central ministries for expenditure on development work in the Northeast have been increased by 110 per cent from ₹36,108 crore in 2014–15 to ₹76,040 crore in 2022–23.

Prime Minister Modi had said, 'For us, the North East and our border areas are not the end points but the gateway to security and prosperity. The security of the nation is also ensured from here and trade and business with other countries also takes place from here. [...] Today, in the North East, we are not drawing borders of disputes, but we are constructing corridors of development; we are emphasizing on that.'[6] This is not a hollow statement but an expression of commitment, well displayed by the way the Northeast is developing. The way relations with South Asia are getting stronger, this gateway will prove to be a milestone in the times to come.

---

[6]'English Rendering of PM's Address at Launch of Various Development Works in Shillong, Meghalaya', *PIBDelhi*, 18 December 2022, https://tinyurl.com/yc8chmay. Accessed on 14 September 2023.

11

DECODING THE 360 DEGREE DEVELOPMENT PUSH

Karma Paljor

The word 'historic' has, over the years, become a victim of being used the way our beloved *dhania* (coriander) is used across the *dhaba*s that form the lifeline of the nation's highways. It is used, more often than not, by people who lack the imagination to conjure words that fit the context. Need a word to make something sound important? Use 'historic'.

With that out of the way, allow me to say: what I witnessed in March 2023 was indeed historic. I am using this word because, well, what I witnessed had never been seen before. And no, I am not talking about unidentified flying objects (UFOs), which is a favourite topic of mine for an evening conversation. I am talking about a crucial piece of infrastructure that many across India now take for granted.

When a Road Is Not Just a Road

On 25 February 2023, Arunachal Pradesh Chief Minister (CM) Pema Khandu drove up to Tali to fulfil a promise he made in 2017. Some wept when they saw the VIP cavalcade enter their village for the first time. 'I felt like crying and cried,' said *gaon bura* Jikke Lonkia from Nobia village, which is half a day's march away. He hoped his village will be connected soon.

Now, the road might be new, but the village is not. Tali was established in 1957 and the fact that it took over 60 years to build a 51-km road must find an entry into the Guinness Book of World Records. The 16,000-odd population waited for development and when it took so long, the majority of them took off to other towns and cities.

'Till about 2007, Airforce AN-32 aircraft used to airdrop ration to Tali,' says Jikke Tako, MLA 20-Tali constituency. It has been a four-year mission for him to get on the road. During elections, helicopters were used. MLA Jikke Tako used to struggle to reach his constituency—walking, crossing the river in a boat and covering the rest of it on tractors and earthmovers.

The road might just be a road. But I, a proud resident of the Northeast and someone, who, like thousands of others, returned to the region to start something of their own, sees this road as a mascot. I see it as a true representation of all that has been achieved and accomplished under the leadership of PM Narendra Modi. Roads connect us to places that hitherto remain distant; in the same way, PM Modi has connected us in ways that seemed impossible until a decade ago.

Furthermore, the road to Tali was not a one-off development. Perhaps the most encouraging trend that we have witnessed in Arunachal Pradesh is that we are no longer 'sleeping' when it comes to developing and protecting our border state. The Border Roads Organisation (BRO) has been playing a significant role in the development of border roads in Arunachal Pradesh under the National Democratic Alliance (NDA) government. The BRO has constructed and upgraded several roads in the state, vastly improving connectivity and accessibility to remote areas. You may have seen videos of supercars vrooming on some of the most picturesque roads in India, but that is not all. The state, under the able leadership of Pema Khandu and the guidance of PM Modi, has undertaken road and infrastructure projects on a war footing. Arunachal is no longer India's 'last' state and its villages are no longer our 'last' villages; instead, they are now our first villages and Arunachal Pradesh is now our first state. All of this has been achieved within 10 years.

Concrete Steps

I am listing a few road projects in Arunachal Pradesh to explain further:

Arunachal Frontier Highway: This is a 2,000-km long road that follows the McMahon Line and connects Mago in Arunachal Pradesh to Vijoynagar near the Myanmar border. The road is being built at a cost of ₹40,000 crore.[1]

Trans-Arunachal Highway: This is a 1,748-km long road starting at Bomdila, connects Tawang in Arunachal Pradesh to Vijoynagar near the Myanmar border. The road is being built at a cost of ₹27,000 crore.[2]

East-West Industrial Corridor Highway: This is a 966.78-km long road along the foothills of Arunachal Pradesh, from Bhairabkunda in West Kameng district, at the trijunction of Bhutan, Assam and Arunachal, to Ruksin in East Siang district, including the existing national highway standard road from Pasighat in East Siang district to Manmao in Changlang district.[3]

These roads have improved connectivity and accessibility to remote areas in Arunachal Pradesh, which has had a positive

---

[1]Philip, Snehesh Alex, 'Modi Govt Moves with Arunachal Frontier Highway, among India's 'Toughest' Projects Yet, China in Mind', *The Print*, 26 November 2022, https://tinyurl.com/mruj73aa. Accessed on 8 December 2023.

[2]Singh, Anamica, 'As LAC Skirmishes Increase, India to Build a 1,700-km Highway in Arunachal Pradesh', *Wion*, 19 December 2022, https://tinyurl.com/yc82n7s2. Accessed on 25 September 2023.

[3]'Arunachal to Take up East-West Industrial Corridor Highway Project with Centre: CM', *The Arunachal Times*, 5 March 2021, https://tinyurl.com/y9evfzmx. Accessed on 25 September 2023.

impact on the socio-economic development of the state. The roads have also made it easier for the Indian Army to deploy troops and equipment in the region, which has enhanced India's security.

In addition to these major projects, the BRO has also constructed and upgraded several other roads in Arunachal Pradesh. These roads have improved connectivity to villages, towns and markets, which has benefited the local population. The roads have also made it easier for the tourists to visit the state, which has boosted the tourism industry.

The NDA government has been committed to improving the infrastructure in Arunachal Pradesh, and the border roads projects are a key part of this effort. These projects have had a significant impact on the state, and they will continue to benefit the people of Arunachal Pradesh for many years to come.

Here are some of the benefits of the border roads project in Arunachal Pradesh under the NDA government:

a) Improved connectivity and accessibility to remote areas
b) Enhanced socio-economic development of the state
c) Strengthened India's security
d) Boosted the tourism industry

More than Marketing: Steps in Infrastructure

You see, as journalists, we often lose sight of the work a government is doing, simply because, truth be told, a detailed story about an upcoming infrastructure project will never get the same reaction as a controversial story on, say, Bollywood actors. However, unlike catchy headlines with shelf lives of less than a day, detailed stories like the one we did from Tali remain etched in the readers' memories for years to come. That is where I believe the NDA government led by the Bharatiya Janata Party (BJP) has made all the difference. Whether it is revolutionizing the telecom sector or improving the public health system—courtesy of world-class institutes like the All India Institute of Medical

Sciences (AIIMS) Guwahati—the changes brought about under PM Modi's leadership will remain for years to come.

Now, I will admit that the Centre has, for decades, tried to work towards connecting the Northeast with not just the rest of India, but also to Southeast Asia. However, it was PM Modi who did it, by simply turning a 'term' into something proactive. 'Look East' became 'Act East' and sure, some might think that this was nothing more than clever marketing. However, as per data, to fulfil this goal, infrastructure development has been a priority under the leadership of PM Modi.

One of the significant initiatives is the Bharatmala Pariyojana. This national highways project, launched in 2015, plans to construct 34,800 km of highways at an estimated cost of ₹5.35 lakh crore.[4] Seven Northeastern towns including Guwahati, Imphal, Silchar, Shillong, Dibrugarh, Dimapur and Aizawl were included in the Bharatmala Pariyojana. The Yojana planned to construct bypasses, ring roads, choke points and congestion points in important cities of the country including the state capitals of Northeastern states to address traffic congestions.[5]

Railway infrastructure has also seen a considerable boost under PM Modi's tenure. This growth is credited to projects like the Bogibeel Bridge, the longest rail-cum-road bridge in India, connecting Assam and Arunachal Pradesh, and the new broad-gauge railway line between Agartala and Sabroom. Manipur is about to get its first full-fledged railway system, and both Mizoram and Nagaland are on course to see railways developing by 2024.[6]

---

[4]Varma, Subodh, 'Highways or Rural Roads, It's a Story of High Cost-Low Delivery', *NewsClick*, 19 August 2023, https://tinyurl.com/54hy3xt7. Accessed on 25 September 2023.

[5]'Seven Cities of Northeast in Bharatmala Pariyojana', *Northeast Now*, 6 August 2018, https://tinyurl.com/3x79xa33. Accessed on 8 December 2023.

[6]'By March 2023, Manipur, Mizoram and Nagaland to Have Rail Connectivity', *Business Standard*, 29 August 2020, https://tinyurl.com/mv5hb7df. Accessed on 8 December 2023.

Many people considered this unachievable until a few years ago.

One aspect that often gets overlooked is the vast improvement in air connectivity to the region. We are no longer limited to picking between five flights a week that only go to two or three state capitals. Under PM Modi's leadership, air connectivity has received substantial attention. By 2023, Ude Desh ka Aam Nagarik (UDAN) scheme launched in 2017 has connected eight capitals of the Northeastern states, which previously had limited or no air connectivity.

Significant focus has also been placed on power infrastructure. The Deendayal Upadhyaya Gram Jyoti Yojana (DDU-GKY) and Integrated Power Development Scheme (IPDS) have been instrumental in electrifying the remote areas of Northeast India.

The Digital India initiative, launched in 2015, aimed to bridge the digital divide in the country. Under this scheme, Northeast India saw the expansion of optical fibre networks to remote regions. Furthermore, the infrastructure development in Northeast India has led to substantial socio-economic transformation. Enhanced road connectivity has boosted trade and tourism, contributing to the region's gross domestic product (GDP). Improved rail and air connectivity has not only made travel easier but has also significantly impacted the economy. The tourism sector, in particular, has benefitted, with the region witnessing a consistent increase in tourist arrivals from 2014 to 2023.

Electrification and digital connectivity initiatives have had a transformative impact on people. With access to electricity, the quality of life has improved, particularly in rural areas. Digital connectivity has opened new avenues for education, healthcare and e-commerce, thereby promoting economic inclusivity.

Unseen Progress: Water and Health

One aspect where I believe the BJP-led NDA government has not gotten the credit it deserves is with regard to tap water supply in the region. The NDA government has made significant achievements in the Northeast with regard to the Jal Jeevan Mission (JJM). This includes:

Water supply: Every Northeast household will get piped water under JJM by 2024. A state like Assam which started with one per cent development, had achieved 54 per cent progress under the mission by July 2023.[7] A grant of ₹9,800 crore had been sanctioned for this purpose.[8] This is a significant achievement, as the region has historically been water-stressed and a rapidly growing population is now threatening traditional sources of water.

Improved water quality: The NDA government has also made significant investments in improving the quality of water in the Northeast. This includes the construction of water treatment plants and the installation of water purification systems.

Increased community participation: The NDA government has also focussed on increasing community participation in the JJM. This has been done through the formation of water user committees and the involvement of local communities in the planning and implementation of the mission.

Maximum coverage: As of September 2023, over 75 per cent of households in the region have access to tap water.[9] The NDA government's achievements in the Northeast under the JJM have had a significant impact on the lives of millions of people. They

---

[7]Kalita, Kangkan, 'Every Northeast Household to Get Piped Water under Jal Jeevan Mission by 2024: Union Minister Gajendra Singh Shekhawat', *The Times of India*, 7 July 2023, https://tinyurl.com/2yshrkpp. Accessed on 8 December 2023.

[8]'Rs 9,800 Crore Allocated to NE States for Jal Jeevan Mission', *Jal Jeevan Mission*, 16 September 2021, https://tinyurl.com/zn2sr29t. Accessed on 8 December 2023.

[9]'Jal Jeevan Mission - Har Ghar Jal', https://tinyurl.com/t3ptazbz. Accessed on 25 September 2023; This is the real-time dashboard. It is safe to assume from here that 75 per cent is the average for the region.

have provided access to safe and clean water, which has improved the health and well-being of people in the region. They have also helped to reduce water-borne diseases and improve agricultural productivity.

Mizoram, Arunachal Pradesh and Nagaland are the best performing states under the JJM. As of September 2023, 93 per cent households in Mizoram, 90 per cent households in Arunachal Pradesh and 78 per cent households in Nagaland have attained access to tap water.[10]

Health has also seen a transformation under the NDA government, with the region reporting much lower casualty during the two painful waves of Covid-19 compared to the rest of the country.

Some of the schemes that have made a huge difference across the Northeast in terms of health, include:

Pradhan Mantri Jan Arogya Yojana (PMJAY): The PMJAY is a government-funded health insurance scheme that provides free or subsidized healthcare to the poor. The scheme has been implemented in Assam. The scheme has provided healthcare to millions of people in the state.

National Health Mission (NHM): The NHM is a government programme that aims to improve the health of people in rural areas. The programme has been implemented in Assam and has helped to improve the quality of healthcare in the state.

National AIDS Control Programme (NACP): The NACP is a government programme that aims to control HIV/AIDS. The programme has been implemented in Assam. It has helped to reduce the spread of HIV/AIDS in the state.

---

[10]Ibid.

Harnessing the Power of Water

We are also painfully aware that climate change is both a reality and inevitable. In such a scenario, I am glad that at least at a policy level, we are seeing so much work being undertaken by the NDA government.

The government has set a target of generating 50 per cent of India's electricity from renewable sources by 2030.[11] The Northeast region is well-positioned to benefit from this, as it has abundant potential for solar, wind and hydropower.

I wish to address hydropower because I believe that the Northeast, especially with Arunachal Pradesh being one of the most hydropower-rich states in India, is a sleeping giant when it comes to producing renewable energy via hydroelectric power. The Brahmaputra River alone accounts for nearly 30 per cent of freshwater resources and 40 per cent of India's hydropower potential. Arunachal Pradesh could be India's apt reservoir to counter China's proposed 60,000 MW hydropower plan in Medog, Tibet.[12]

The NDA government has taken a number of steps to promote hydropower development in the state. For example, the government has streamlined the clearance process for hydropower projects, which has helped to speed up the development of these projects. The government has provided financial assistance to a number of hydropower projects in Arunachal Pradesh, which has helped to make these projects more feasible. Under the leadership of PM Modi, the government has encouraged public-private partnerships for hydropower development, which has helped to attract private

---

[11]'PTI, India on Track to Have 50 PC Installed Power Capacity via Non-Fossil Fuel Sources: R K Singh', *Energyworld.com*, 5 December 2023, https://tinyurl.com/2n4nksku. Accessed on 8 December 2023.

[12]Koshy, Jacob, 'India Plans 'Buffers' in Proposed Arunachal Hydropower Project to Counter "China Threat"', *The Hindu*, 17 January 2023, https://tinyurl.com/2s3u34k8. Accessed on 8 December 2023.

investment in this sector. As a result of these efforts, hydropower development in Arunachal Pradesh has accelerated under the NDA government. A number of large hydropower projects have been completed or are under construction in the state, and the government is targeting an installed capacity of 30,000 MW by 2030.[13]

Some of the most spectacular undertakings include the 600 MW Kameng hydropower project, which was dedicated to the nation by PM Modi in 2018.[14] The Indian government has approved the 2,800 MW Dibang Multipurpose Project in 2023. The nine year project bordering China will stand on an estimated investment of ₹1,600 crore.[15]

The development of hydropower in Arunachal Pradesh is expected to have a number of benefits for the state, including helping to increase electricity generation in Arunachal Pradesh, which will help to meet the growing demand for electricity in the state. It will create jobs in the construction and operation of hydropower projects and will help to boost economic development in Arunachal Pradesh by providing a source of clean and renewable energy.

Climate Consciousness

Other efforts to tackle climate change include promoting sustainable agriculture. The government is working to help farmers in the Northeast to adopt more sustainable agricultural practices. This includes promoting the use of climate-resilient

---

[13]'Prime Minister Shri Narendra Modi Dedicates to the Nation the 600 MW Kameng Hydro Power Station Implemented by Neepco Ltd., a Mini Ratna Power PSU under Ministry of Power', *PIBDelhi*, 19 November 2022, https://tinyurl.com/3abnf87m. Accessed on 8 December 2023.

[14]Ibid.

[15]'Govt Approves $3.9 Billion Hydropower Project near China Border', *Livemint*, 28 February 2023, https://tinyurl.com/mr2f8d2n. Accessed on 8 December 2023.

crops, water-efficient irrigation methods and organic farming. Further, forests play an important role in mitigating climate change. The government is working to protect forests in the Northeast by creating new protected areas and enforcing forest laws. Funds from the National Mission for Green India (GIM) will flow in 90:10 ratio for the Northeast of India.[16] The programme is expected to help mitigate climate change, improve air quality and conserve water.

The government is also investing in infrastructure that is more resilient to the impacts of climate change. This includes building roads, bridges and dams that can withstand floods and landslides.

The North East Climate Change Adaptation Programme (NECCAP) is a government programme that aims to help the Northeast region adapt to the impacts of climate change. The programme is expected to help improve the region's water management, agricultural practices and disaster risk management.

In conclusion, one can safely say that PM Modi's persistent all-around efforts and initiatives have significantly improved the standard of living in the Northeastern states.

---

[16]Sharma, Yogima, 'Mission for Green India, MGNREGA Will Converge to Facilitate Afforestation on 10 Million Hectares of Land', *The Economic Times*, 9 March 2015, https://tinyurl.com/3pzphhnt. Accessed on 8 December 2023.

12

PUBLIC HEALTH IN THE NORTHEAST

Aashish Chandorkar

On Sunday, 4 October 2021, a black and white helicopter-shaped unmanned aircraft took off from the Bishnupur district hospital premises in Manipur. Its destination was the public health centre located in the Karang Island, situated on the Loktak lake.[1] A large freshwater lake which can vary in size from 250 sq. km to 500 sq. km depending on the rains, Loktak has islands or *phumdis,* some of which float on top of the water. These islands have small habitations that are tough to reach.

The unmanned aircraft from Bishnupur was carrying Covid-19 vaccines for the people who are part of the lake's ecosystem. Bearing the insignia of the made-in-India start-ups like Daybest, Helicam India, Model Aviation and the premier health research organization—Indian Council of Medical Research (ICMR)—the vaccine delivery was successfully demonstrated. The aerial distance covered was less than half the road distance and the time required was cut by a sixth.[2]

This was an example of how the Narendra Modi government

---

[1]'Drones Start Covid Vaccines Delivery in Northeast, Make First Drop In Manipur', *The Print*, 4 October 2021, https://tinyurl.com/s7npm68d. Accessed 14 September 2023.

[2]Jha, Devesh, *LinkedIn*, https://tinyurl.com/2r6bx736. Accessed on 14 September 2023.

worked on rapid vaccination across the country, coordinating the availability, accessibility and affordability of these vaccines using indigenous strengths and capacities. The last-mile vaccine delivery was especially a challenge in the Northeast region due to the tough terrain. This is especially a challenge for products like vaccines that need special handling as well as skills for site administration.

Public Vaccination: A Challenging Task

India's public vaccination programme for Covid-19, administered more than 2.2 billion doses[3] while also exporting more than 300 million doses to other countries.[4] The programme achieved amongst the highest coverage of target population, with more than 90 per cent of adults receiving their first dose in just over a year into the vaccination programme.[5]

This was not just better coverage than significantly more-endowed countries of the West, but it was doubly satisfying—given India's inherent socioeconomic, cultural and geographic differences. The vaccination journey had to overcome three very specific structural issues—movement of people within states and within the country, tough-to-access terrains and vaccine hesitancy amid the masses. These challenges were more visible in India's Northeast.

When the government set its heart on 100 per cent vaccine coverage, it had to first look at population estimates at district, block and village level to fine-tune the vaccine supply chain. In the Northeast, migration is routine. The migration can be to states

---

[3]See more at: *Ministry of Health and Family Welfare, Government of India*, https://tinyurl.com/436vr662. Accessed 25 June 2023.

[4]'Vaccine Supply', *Ministry of External Affairs, Government of India*, 15 June 2023, https://tinyurl.com/2vhk92ff. Accessed 14 September 2023.

[5]Chandorkar, Aashish, and Suraj Sudhir, *Braving A Viral Storm: India's Covid-19 Vaccine Story*, Rupa Publications, 2023.

in the region, the states around the country and the big cities—especially the capital cities in the same state. Since the last census data was from 2011, with the 2021 census postponed due to the pandemic, estimation for vaccine supplies to be made available in the states needed additional work.

The geography in the Ashta Lakshmi states is amongst the most complex in the country. Think of any daunting geographic feature and one finds it in this region. From the mighty Himalayas to majestic rivers, from landlocked states with limited road and rail access to a few airstrips often impacted by bad weather, it is not easy to move around, especially when the vaccine consignments had to move with specific transportation requirements.

Finally, there was the barrier of vaccine hesitancy. In November 2021, 49 districts had reported vaccination coverage of less than 50 per cent. Twenty-seven of these were in the Northeast region. Kiphire district in Nagaland had approximately 16.1 per cent coverage, Kangkopki was at 17.1 per cent and Kra Daadi district in Arunachal Pradesh had around 18.3 per cent coverage.[6] The hesitancy had its roots in a mix of myths about the vaccine, religious beliefs and opinions of local influencers.

Three-Pronged Approach

The government worked hard on all these issues from the triple A lens—Availability, Accessibility and Affordability.

The vaccines were made available and accessible, overcoming the logistical barriers. The cold chains, which leveraged the knowhow of Mission Indradhanush launched by the Modi government early in its first term, helped to build confidence that the vaccines would be available in sufficient quantities in all the locations required. Innovations like drone delivery further

---

[6]Mehta, Payal, 'Migration, Myths and Mountains: Chief Ministers Explain Low Vaccine Coverage in the Northeast', *News18,* 2 November 2021, https://tinyurl.com/ye223m3z. Accessed on 14 September 2023.

bolstered the view that the government was serious about Mission Antodaya[7] reaching every person in the society.

There were local innovations like mobile vans going from door to door to coax and cajole citizens into taking their vaccine dose or completing the two-course doses.[8] The Har Ghar Dastak (meaning 'knock every door') programme launched by Union Health Minister Mansukh Mandaviya especially helped in pushing the vaccine coverage in this region.

The use of the national CoWIN digital platform for data management on vaccines ensured that the second dose of the vaccine could be taken anywhere in the country, in any central government facility. This greatly helped those working outside their home states, as they did not have to worry about missing or delaying their second dose if they had taken the first dose in a location different from their work location.

To ensure that the issues related to hesitancy were addressed, the Prime Minister (PM) himself held direct dialogues with district officials[9] to understand localized concerns and then design solutions that could work in the specific social context.

India's Covid-19 vaccine programme remained free for those who chose to use the free vaccine facilities. Eventually, the vaccine coverage in the eight states caught up to keep the society at large safe from the mutations and variations of the deadly virus.

The interventions made by the government during the health emergency were in continuation of how the Modi government

---

[7]Mission Antyodaya is a convergence and accountability framework aiming to bring optimum use and management of resources allocated by 27 Ministries/ Department of the Government of India under various programmes for the development of rural areas. It is envisaged as a state-led initiative with Gram Panchayats as focal points of convergence efforts. See more at: *Mission Antodaya*, https://tinyurl.com/yj6mcvam. Accessed on 5 December 2023.

[8]Mehta, Payal, 'Migration, Myths and Mountains: Chief Ministers Explain Low Vaccine Coverage in the Northeast', *News18*, 2 November 2021, https://tinyurl.com/ye223m3z. Accessed on 14 September 2023.

[9]Ibid.

has maintained a razor-sharp focus on the healthcare systems in the Northeast. The states in this region are relatively poor, have seen social conflicts and turmoil and were less connected to the national mainstream. The government had been addressing these issues since long before the pandemic arrived.

Florence Nightingale and Beyond

For a very long time, the healthcare and sanitation situation in India has had big gaps. In fact, the British colonial government had designated a 'Royal Commission appointed to Inquire into Regulations affecting the Sanitary Conditions of Army, the Organization of Military Hospitals, and the Treatment of the Sick and Wounded' in 1857–58. This commission was headed by Florence Nightingale, demonstrating how even the colonial overlords pegged importance to the subject, even if for a narrow end of improving the health conditions of its own armies and soldiers.[10] While India has come a long way since that time, the spatial and the temporal distribution of healthcare facilities has been far from uniform.

The book *Bridgital Nation*, authored by N. Chandrasekaran and Roopa Purushothaman, starts with the story of Nikhil Burman from Silchar, Assam. Burman, a driver, would wait on a National Highway for patients coming from various parts of the Northeastern states, seeking better treatment, mostly in Assam. Burman, not trained in any medical skills, would check the patient and advise them which hospital they should go to.[11]

It would appear that between Florence Nightingale's report and Nikhil Burman's 'experience-based' first diagnosis, not a lot had changed at least for this region.

---

[10]Aiyar, Shankkar, *The Gated Republic: India's Public Policy Failures and Private Solutions*, HarperCollins Publishers India, 2020.

[11]Chandrasekaran, N., and Roopa Purushothaman, *Bridgital Nation: Solving Technology's People Problem*, Penguin Random House India Private Limited, 2019.

An acute health issue in the Northeast has been the spread of cancer, resulting mainly from the high level of consumption of tobacco and related products. The Assam Cancer Care Foundation, set up in 2017, sought to combat the deadly and dispiriting gaze of cancer. This foundation is a joint partnership between the Government of Assam and Tata Trusts.[12]

The foundation has brought to the fore a new three-tier model for cancer care, seeking to bring standardized and affordable treatment to the patients' homes. The foundation has set up one apex centre, supplemented with several level two and level three centres. These second and third-tier centres are spread across the state.

This design helps patients in earlier, easier and cheaper diagnosis of the disease. The load is shifted from the few specialized hospitals in the capital and big cities. Basic treatment can be given in the level three centres, while level two centres provide higher degree of specialization and greater care facilities. The apex centre is reserved for interventions which have to be dealt at super-speciality level.

Assam: Developing Medical Infrastructure

Assam being the largest state in the region is the preferred healthcare destination for those in other states too. Recent upgrade in cancer care facilities has been supplemented by planned improvement in treating cardiovascular diseases. The Assam government signed a memorandum of understanding (MoU) with a Rajkot-based organization called Prashanti Medical Services & Research Foundation, which will help undertake 1,000 heart surgeries—500 each for adults and children over

---

[12]See more at: *Assam Cancer Care Foundation*, https://tinyurl.com/4r7j7uxv. Accessed 7 June 2023.

the next two years.[13] Such ingenious ideas are fast confronting the stasis of the past decades.

It is not just these public-private collaborations that have come to the fore. The fundamental issue of medical infrastructure itself is being resolved. It took Assam 60 years after independence to get to a count of four medical colleges. However, four new medical colleges have come up just in a short period after the pandemic crisis. This has been facilitated by the National Medical Commission reforms undertaken by the Modi government.[14]

Assam now boasts over 10 medical colleges, including a private college and an All India Institute of Medical Sciences (AIIMS).[15] The central government has invested ₹1,123 crore in the AIIMS project, a super-specialty hospital, which aims to benefit the entire region.[16]

On the day the AIIMS was inaugurated, PM Modi also laid the foundation of Assam Advanced Health Innovation Institute (AAHII), a ₹546-crore joint initiative of the state government and IIT Guwahati. This institute will promote research, innovation and inventions in medicine focussing on multidisciplinary capabilities at the confluence of engineering and medicine.[17]

---

[13]'New Era in Assam's Healthcare Sector', *The Sentinel*, 9 January 2023, https://tinyurl.com/bdzfwnv9. Accessed on 14 September 2023.

[14]Kalita, Kangkan, 'Assam Takes 60 Years to Get 4 Medical Colleges but 1 Year to Get 4 Running', *The Times Of India*, 16 March 2023, https://tinyurl.com/363e8m2n. Accessed 14 September 2023.

[15]'Medical Colleges in Assam 2024-25: MBBS, Govt & Private Medical Colleges Etc.', *Edufever*, 29 November 2023, https://tinyurl.com/ysrxx565. Accessed on 14 September 2023.

[16]PTI, 'PM Modi Dedicates Northeast's First AIIMS, Three New Medical Colleges in Assam', *The Economic Times*, 14 April 2023, https://tinyurl.com/wyf9rrze. Accessed on 14 September 2023.

[17]Ibid.

Taking up the Reins of Development

The central government has provided 90 per cent funding for eight medical colleges in this region. Each college is setup with a corpus of ₹189 crore. Of this, ₹170 crore come from the central government. Apart from the four colleges in Assam—in Dhubri, Nagaon, North Lakhimpur and Diphu, plans are afoot to set up new medical colleges in other states too. Two colleges in Naharlagun in Arunachal Pradesh and Falkawn in Mizoram have been completed while those in West Garo Hills in Meghalaya and a Naga Hospital in Nagaland are work in progress.[18] In fact, the first batch of medical graduates from the Mizoram's medical college completed its coursework in April 2023, bringing new hopes to the state.[19]

The hospital project in Nagaland was approved in February 2014. However, the funds were released in February 2019. The Nagaland Institute of Medical Sciences and Research (NIMSR) at Phriebagei, Kohima is expected to start functioning soon, reaching its intended capacity in the next three years. In addition, assistance also came from the Japan International Cooperation Agency (JICA) in funding the medical college.[20]

This focus and the prioritization of bringing quality healthcare to every state in the Northeast is showing results. Medical colleges in Tripura have been doing commendable work under the National Tuberculosis Eradication Programme (NTEP). Patient enrolment, scanning for comorbidities and research and training

---

[18]Kalita, Kangkan, "'Centre Bore 90% Project Cost for 8 New Medical Colleges In Northeast'", *The Times of India*, 11 December 2022, https://tinyurl.com/bdz98t7c. Accessed on 14 September 2023.

[19]'First Batch of Mizoram's Only Medical College Completes Their MBBS Course, New Medical Graduates Hope to Improve Healthcare in the State', *OpIndia*, 14 April 2023, https://tinyurl.com/yv5s44fe. Accessed on 14 September 2023.

[20]'Nagaland CM Rio Assures Additional Funding for State's First Medical College', *The Morung Express*, 20 June 2023, https://tinyurl.com/48dyazyx. Accessed on 14 September 2023.

on tuberculosis—another national and regional health obstacle—have shown improvements in the state.[21]

These developments bring hope to a beautiful region of India, which holds high potential with excellent human capital but has not been able to transform its potential energy to the kinetic benefits of economic growth and development. Improved health outcomes could be critical inputs into this journey, addressing the root cause of poverty and unrealized possibilities.

In the story of Nikhil Burman in *Bridgital Nation,* a few years ago, when these interventions had not shaped up, Burman tells one of his 'patients' from Tripura: 'But if you die (there), I will not send your body back to Tripura. I will arrange for you to be cremated here.'[22] This highlights the stark contrast between the conditions of healthcare facilities then and in recent times.

The developments of the recent years hold a ray of hope that such *fait accompli* will not be presented to the population of the Northeast. The words of PM Modi from his speech at the inauguration of AIIMS, Guwahati underlined this home, 'I am happy that today the people of the North East have taken upon themselves the reins of development. They are moving forward with the mantra of the development of North East to India's development.'[23]

---

[21]Chakraborty, Tanmoy, 'Medical Colleges in Tripura Secure Top Position in Northeast for National Tuberculosis Eradication Program', *India Today NE*, 30 May 2023, https://tinyurl.com/at97h87w. Accessed on 14 September 2023.

[22]Chandrasekaran, N., and Roopa Purushothaman, *Bridgital Nation: Solving Technology's People Problem*, Penguin Random House India Private Limited, 2019.

[23]'Our Government Is Modernizing India's Health Sector According to the Needs of the 21st Century: PM Modi', *Narendra Modi*, 14 April 2023, https://tinyurl.com/4tr4m4cx. Accessed on 14 September 2023.

13

ACCELERATING FINANCIAL INCLUSION

Dinesh Nandwana

The North Eastern Region (NER) has a population of approximately five crore with an area of more than 2.6 lakh sq. km. A large portion of this population had been previously excluded from the easy access to financial services. Access to finance, especially by the poor and marginalized section of the population, is a prerequisite for creating employment opportunities, economic growth, poverty reduction and social cohesion. For most people around the world, having an account in a formal financial institution serves as an entry point into the formal financial sector.

Over the last decade, the acceleration of financial inclusion in India has been largely due to political will along with high-impact initiatives by the Modi government, such as the Pradhan Mantri Jan Dhan Yojana (PMJDY), social security schemes, direct benefit transfer (DBT) and the issue of RuPay cards, among others.

The Modi government recognized the need to integrate a biometric ID system (Aadhaar) into two other pillars for reforms: mobile communications and financial access. The resulting trinity is known as JAM—Jan Dhan (financial inclusion), Aadhaar and Mobile.

As per latest data, PMJDY accounts have crossed 50 crore and deposits now exceed two lakh crore.[1]

The government has followed a three-step approach to achieve its goal of financial inclusion. First, it has provided universal access to banking facilities by opening 'no frills' accounts for the masses. Second, it has brought and retained people in the financial system through initiatives like digital payments and promoting the use of RuPay cards. Third, it has focussed on creating the necessary infrastructure by increasing the reach and accessibility of financial services. Through its conducive policies, the government is promoting banking correspondents, white label ATMs (WLAs) and digital payments. As a result, a new generation of financial services accessible through mobile phones and the internet has emerged in the country.

Initiatives such as the PMJDY has been put in place with the objective of ensuring access to various financial services like availability of basic savings bank account, access to need based credit, remittances facility, insurance and pension to the excluded sections i.e., weaker sections and low-income groups. This deep penetration at affordable cost is possible only with effective use of technology.

The plan also envisages channelling all government benefits (from the Centre, state and local bodies) to the beneficiaries' accounts and pushing the DBT scheme of the Union Government.

Financial and Social Inclusion Initiatives

The NER witnessed a paradigm shift in the financial and social inclusion initiatives. The number of no-frills zero balance bank accounts opened under PMJDY scheme has been at 2.62 crore and the number of RuPay cards issued to beneficiaries is 1.43 crore; the total balance amount in these accounts stood at ₹7,658

---

[1]'PMJDY Accounts Cross 50 Crore, Deposits Exceed `2 Lakh Crore', *The Hindu*, 26 August 2023, https://tinyurl.com/zb8s7udx. Accessed on 25 September 2023.

crore as of March 2023. More than ₹31,600 crore of DBT subsidies have been transferred in these accounts in the last financial year (FY) 2023 (see table below).

Table 1[2]
Financial and Social Inclusion Initiatives: Performance Achievements (As on 26 April 2023 since 2014)

PMJDY	Pan India	NER
No. of PMJDY Accounts	48.84 crore	2.62 crore
Total Deposits	₹197,936 crore	₹7,658 crore
No. of RuPay Cards Issued		1.43 crore
DBT		
Total DBT (Cumulative)	₹2,976,649 crore	
Total DBT (FY 2022–23)	₹708,613 crore	₹31,606 crore
Pradhan Mantri Suraksha Bima Yojana (PMSBY) Enrolment	34.18 crore policy holders	
Pradhan Mantri Jeevan Jyoti Bima Yojana (PMJJBY) Enrolment	16.19 crore policy holders	
Atal Pension Yojana (APY) Enrolment	5.24 crore pension policy holders	

Under the leadership of Prime Minister (PM) Narendra Modi, the NER has witnessed a major improvement in the banking infrastructure along with the accessibility to finance made available for economic growth. More than 2,000 scheduled commercial bank branches opened in the NER in the last nine years (2014–2022) as compared to 851 branches opened in the previous 10 years (2004–2013). There has been robust improvement in the per capita income of the people as well as an increase in the credit growth by 85 per cent.

[2]See more at: *Direct Benefit Transfer, Government of India,* http://tinyurl.om/kes3ubuy. Accessed on 18 September 2023.

Table 2
Update On Banking Infrastructure in the NER[3]

Number of total bank branches of scheduled commercial banks in NER (FY 2004)	**1,918**
Number of total bank branches of scheduled commercial banks in NER (FY 2022)	**4,799**
Number of branches added between 2004–2013	**851**
Number of branches added between 2014–2022	**1,670**

In its financial inclusion drive, the government is also supported by various private sector players. Private entities such as various business correspondents and WLA operators have delivered service innovations by providing Bio-metric enabled Interoperable banking (AEPS) and WLA services through a technology-driven platform. They have managed to boost rural entrepreneurship, increase the level of financial literacy and leverage their presence by becoming an integral part of the supply chain for e-commerce and other companies waiting to tap into the rural market.

Even during the crisis situation of the Covid-19 pandemic followed by the lockdown in the country, business correspondents and WLAs were operational even with extended working hours to provide access to the key essential services and thus serving the people in the Northeast. For example, players like Vakrangee, a business correspondent and a WLA operator, were fully operational during the lockdown and provided key emergency and essential services to the citizens. During the pandemic, Vakrangee had opened more than 19,300 bank accounts in the NER. The company's gross transaction value (GTV) (cash deposits/withdrawals) crossed ₹143 crore and the number of transactions crossed 6.3 lakhs in the NER through its banking

---

[3]'Table 143: State-Wise Distribution of Offices of Scheduled Commercial Banks', *rbi.org*, https://tinyurl.com/3axv7fm8. Accessed on 18 September 2023.

and ATM services during the last financial year FY 2023.[4]

I am putting forth a few case studies to elucidate how we, along with government support, have made digital inclusion a reality in some of the most remote areas of the NER and this positive intervention has transformed individual lives for the better.

Case study 1

Anowar Hussain (business correspondent)

- Number of bank accounts opened: 4,062
- Village: Ghilajari, Assam
- Location: Tier 6
- Gram Panchayat: Hazipara
- District: Barpeta

The citizens of Gilajari village situated in gram panchayat Hazipara, earlier used to travel long distances for their basic financial and banking needs as the nearest branches of State Bank of India (SBI) and ICICI Bank were situated more than 10 km away. Through the Vakrangee Kendra business correspondents outlet, local citizens have been able to get access to financial and social inclusion services such as banking, DBT of subsidies as well as insurance and pension services. Further, the outlet opens for 12 hours a day, thereby providing access to extended banking hours. The banking services provided are completely digital, paperless and biometric-enabled. Citizens are able to open free zero balance accounts and can deposit and withdraw cash without any charges within the local neighbourhood.

Local micro, small and medium enterprises (MSME) such as retail store vendors, vegetable vendors and others have opened their bank accounts and are using QR code-enabled UPI (unified payments interface) transactions for payments to their suppliers. Their payments are settled in real time and they are able to

---

[4]The figures presented regarding Vakrangee are privy to the author.

earn monthly interest on the savings in their bank accounts. This is truly changing the landscape of how rural economy works in the Northeast and is an example of digital inclusion in a true sense.

Case study 2

Gopal Barman (business correspondent)

- Number of accounts opened: 1,922
- Village: Panka Gaon
- Location: Tier 6
- Gram Panchayat: Panka
- District: Golaghat

The Golaghat district being an industrial belt has majority of the unserved population working as labour class. The village, Panka Gaon has five to six bank branches within a 10 km radius. These customers, who are largely from the labour class, have been deprived of access to banking services at most bank branches. This is partially due to the fact that they do not form the priority customer base for the bank branches. There is also the limitation of low literacy levels, which makes filling physical forms and other documentation a challenge for them.

The business correspondent banking outlet provided free zero balance account opening services along with no maintenance charges. Furthermore, entire banking services are biometric-enabled and paperless, requiring no physical documentation. This makes the services more accessible to this group of customers.

These business correspondent outlets and WLAs have led to an emergence of a strong last mile infrastructure in the rural NER and provided universal access to the government's financial inclusion initiatives. It has led to larger financial and digital inclusion drive in the local neighbourhood. As a result, local vendors and MSMEs such as pan shops, grocery shops and others have also opened bank accounts and enabled QR Codes/UPI for digital payments.

Distribution of DBT Subsidy

Through the vast network of banking business correspondents and WLA outlets, the government is driving financial, digital and social inclusion in unserved and underserved locations in rural India. The ultimate purpose is to ensure that every Indian citizen has the opportunity to benefit from financial, digital and social inclusion and has access to the global marketplace.

Our organization feels privileged to have contributed in the government efforts at maximising financial inclusion in the NER. We are delivering real-time banking and financial services, ATMs, insurance, e-governance, e-commerce and total healthcare services to the unserved rural and semi-urban markets. The company currently has 20,399 outlets spread across 29 states and union territories, 79 per cent outlets in tier 4 and 6 locations. The company currently has 110 outlets in the NER spread across 34 districts and 75 postal codes.

By 2030, our company plans to have 100 per cent coverage of the NER through its outlet network along with the Bharat Easy digital mobile app. The target is to reach over 50,000 outlets spread across each and every gram panchayat and village of the NER.

14

CARVING A NICHE FOR *NARI SHAKTI*: THE MODI WAY

Phangnon Konyak

Women across the country have been major players in catapulting the Bharatiya Janata Party (BJP) to power since 2014.[1] This is both at the Centre and the state level. Women have been the mainstay of BJP, all for good reasons. Ever since Narendra Modi became the Prime Minister (PM), he has been on a mission to empower the women of India like never before. He has emphasized on *nari shakti* (women power) to take the country forward. From the ramparts of the Red Fort during the 74th Independence Day celebrations, he spoke about several issues of societal importance and relevance. The PM took the lead in shattering some taboos by talking about menstruation in a first of its kind gesture by any PM of the country. The mention was meant to relieve the citizens from the tradition of embarrassment and celebrate the unstoppable female forces emerging and establishing themselves in leadership positions with fierce determination. Prime Minister Modi has been at the forefront of enabling this change.

[1]Ranjan, Ashish, 'Assembly Election Results 2023: Why BJP's Footprint Is Growing in the Northeast', *India Today*, 3 March 2023, https://tinyurl.com/4v7ymbh8. Accessed on 18 September 2023.

Clean Fuel and Rations

Many factors can be attributed to this change. Welfare policies and schemes of the Modi government have been vital in bringing our women to the fore in the cause of nation building. It is the case in our very own state of Nagaland. The impact is there for everyone to see. The Pradhan Mantri Ujjwala Yojana (PMUY), which aims to safeguard the health of women and children by providing clean cooking fuel, is a roaring success in the state. It is our sisters and mothers in the rural areas and villages who stand to benefit the most. They no longer have to go in search of firewood, which was both dangerous and inconvenient. What's more assuring is the fact that, connections are issued under the name of the women of the household. In fact, the BJP Mahila Morcha in Nagaland has helped facilitate numerous LPG (liquefied petroleum gas) connections under the scheme. The days of spending time in the smoky kitchen and exposing oneself to health problems are long gone.

The Pradhan Mantri Garib Kalyan Anna Yojana (PMGKAY) is another welfare scheme that has had maximum impact on the welfare of not only women but on the society as a whole. This effect was clearly visible during the times of the Covid-19 pandemic. Thousands of families across Nagaland were saved from starvation during this horrid period, thanks to the free ration scheme. It is the world's largest food security programme and has been crucial towards ensuring food security.[2]

The Pradhan Mantri Awas Yojana (PMAY) also deserves a special mention. It has not only ensured a roof over the head but also the dignity of women. The Pradhan Mantri Awas Yojana–Urban [PMAY (U)] has made a mandatory provision for the female head of the family to be the owner or co-owner of

---

[2]Tripathy, Ram Prasad, 'PMGKAY - Largest Food Security Programme in the World', *Kamal Sandesh*, 14 December 2021, https://tinyurl.com/3e7wrnev. Accessed on 18 September 2023.

the house. Over 32,000 beneficiaries in Nagaland now have access to affordable housing. This is only possible due to the visionary leadership of PM Modi, who has made it his personal mission to empower women of the country on a war footing.

Another scheme making waves is Sukanya Samriddhi Yojana (SSY) which is a government savings scheme created with the intention to benefit the girl child under the initiative of Beti Bachao Beti Padhao. Under this initiative, the parent or guardian of a girl child who is 10 years of age or younger can open an account. The account carries a high interest rate along with several tax benefits. One can apply for Sukanya Samriddhi Account scheme through the post offices or participating public and private banks. In fact, on 25 September 2020, state BJP President Temjen Imna Along kicked off the BJP Mahila Morcha Nagaland initiative to help open at least 100 Sukanya Samriddhi accounts in each district.

Improving Women's Lives

Through these small ways, the party has been trying to take the Modi government's welfare policies to the people. With over 2.3 lakh households as beneficiaries, Nagaland is well on its way towards universal health coverage, courtesy of Ayushman Bharat Pradhan Mantri Jan Arogya Yojana (AB-PMJAY)[3]. A huge percentage of the beneficiaries are women who are now able to access affordable treatment and healthcare insurance. The flagship Jal Jeevan Mission (JJM) has also been instrumental in saving time, energy and resources of our women. The burden of having to fetch water has been mitigated. These are just some of the ways in which women have benefitted because of the comprehensive policies of the Modi government. The PM himself has been vocal and active in this mission, to inspire more believers and work

---

[3]See more at: *Ayushman Bharat Pradhan Mantri Jan Arogya Yojana*, https://tinyurl.com/4vaaubj9. Accessed on 25 September 2023.

towards bigger results crossing all barriers in empowering women.

For the first time in the state's history, we have two women legislators in Nagaland. In the state assembly polls held in five states in 2022, the BJP came to power in four, and it was found that more women than men have voted for the BJP.[4] The party has earned its goodwill and the trust of sisters with sincerity, diligence and hard work. Things have changed since 2014. Be it sanitation, menstrual hygiene, tap water connection or cooking gas, the BJP has succeeded in making women-centric issues its priority.

The future is only going to get better for the women of our country. With PM Modi increasingly focusing on women taking on combat roles in the Navy and Air Force, it does not take much to gauge the seriousness of the present government and its respect for women-power. What's even more assuring is that the country is continuously seeing women leaders on the rise in New India. Droupadi Murmu assuming the responsibility as the first tribal President of India speaks volumes of the Modi government's commitment towards gender equality along with its efforts in uplifting the country's tribal population.

Women over the country and region, including our Naga mothers and sisters, are looking ahead towards the future with optimism. The country is changing for the better. Women are now the driving force behind the country's quest for progress and development, and with the Northeast getting focussed attention and more economic opportunities, I think it's safe to say that we will be shouldering bigger responsibilities in the days to come, ones that are not necessarily limited to the confines of our homes.

---

[4]Ranjan, Ashish, 'Assembly Election Results 2023: Why BJP's Footprint Is Growing in the Northeast', *India Today*, 3 March 2023, https://tinyurl.com/4v7ymbh8. Accessed on 18 September 2023.

15

NURTURING THE SEED: THE START-UP ECOSYSTEM

K. Karthikeyen
Uday Wankawala

The North Eastern Region (NER) of India is a land of breathtaking landscapes, diverse cultures and rich biodiversity. However, despite its abundant resources and potential, the region has long remained untapped in terms of economic growth and development. In the current times, one of the critical avenues for catalysing growth in the region is through the establishment of a robust start-up and entrepreneurial ecosystem. Prime Minister (PM) Narendra Modi, at the inaugural session of the Assam Global Investors' Summit, held on 3–4 February 2018 in Guwahati, said that the Northeast is at the heart of the Union government's Act East Policy. The Act East Policy envisions increased people to people contact, trade ties and other relations with the Association of Southeast Asian Nations (ASEAN).

The NER comprises eight states—Arunachal Pradesh, Assam, Manipur, Meghalaya, Mizoram, Nagaland, Sikkim and Tripura. Historically, the region has faced infrastructural, connectivity and administrative challenges that have hindered its economic progress. This, coupled with the predominantly agrarian economy and a lack of industrialization, has resulted in a mindset that leans towards risk aversion. Under the leadership of PM Modi, the region has taken major steps to give impetus to the ecosystem by creating innovation hubs and engaging the youth through universities, Atal Tinkering Laboratories (ATLs) under the Atal Innovation Mission including the Atal Incubation Centres (AIC) and Bio Incubation Centres under the BioNest scheme; launching entrepreneurial skill-based programmes; and funding through various government schemes like Startup India Seed Fund Schemes (SISFS). Another example is the North East Venture Fund (NEVF), which has been established to support start-ups in the region by providing them with early-stage funding. This fund was created to encourage entrepreneurship and innovation in the Northeast.

Opportunities and Initiatives

In the context of various steps towards development, it must be kept in mind that the NER presents several unique opportunities that, if harnessed effectively, will transform the start-up landscape:

Cultural diversity: The rich cultural diversity of the NER can serve as an asset in fostering innovation. Different perspectives can lead to creative solutions that cater to a wider audience.

Natural resources and traditional knowledge: The region's vast natural resources and traditional knowledge can be the basis for sustainable and eco-friendly start-ups. Sectors like agro-processing, cash crops such as tea, coffee, spices; traditional handicrafts, climate change, smart agriculture and alternate medicine hold significant potential.

Tourism and hospitality: The NER's picturesque landscapes and diverse cultures can be leveraged to develop a thriving tourism and hospitality start-up ecosystem. Combining the efforts of the local community and the youth, entrepreneurs could leverage the potential that tourism promises.

Digital connectivity: Improvements in digital infrastructure, including the spread of mobile internet, present opportunities for online businesses and tech start-ups. Start-ups that use technology as an enabler for traditional sectors such as agriculture and biotech, find traction in scaling and disrupting traditional market practices.

Youth demographic: The NER has a youthful population, which can be a driving force for entrepreneurship. Fostering entrepreneurial education and skill development among the youth will yield positive outcomes. Most youth in the NER are literate, agile, aspirational, coachable and eager to learn.

Building a Support System: Schemes and Institutions

To extend the required support, agencies promoting entrepreneurship in the region have been set up with assistance from the Centre and the State/s. Simply put, the start-up culture prevalent in the rest of India and the global stage needs to be replicated in the region. Business incubators play a pivotal role towards this to support such entities and help in the development of entrepreneurship in this region.

An incubation centre is an entity that provides a host of services including business mentoring, seed funding, marketing support, access to technical experts and physical co-working spaces for entrepreneurs and start-ups.

A few of the active incubators and institutions working in the entrepreneurship development domain are Assam Agricultural University Incubator (AAU; also known as the North East Agriculture Technology Entrepreneurs Hub [NEATeHub]); Assam Startup The Nest; Indian Institute of Entrepreneurship (IIE); Science & Technological Intervention for North East India (STINER); Assam Agribusiness Growth Lab (AAGL); Guwahati Biotech Park (GBP), Institute of Advanced Study in Science and Technology

(IASST); and CSIR-NEIST Bioincubator. The AIC–AAU incubator is an agri-tech incubator supported and funded by the AIM of NITI Aayog, as well as the Rashtriya Krishi Vikas Yojana-Remunerative Approaches for Agriculture and Allied Sectors Rejuvenation (RKVY-RAFTAAR) introduced by the Ministry of Agriculture and Farmers' Welfare (MoA&FW). Most entrepreneurs are founders of agri-based start-ups with small teams who are supported by NEATeHub through a host of services such as business mentoring, seed funding, marketing support, access to technical experts, physical co-working spaces, etc. Similarly, AIC-Rambhau Mhalgi Prabodhini (RMP) foundation based in Uttan, Thane, Maharashtra, is supported by AIM, NITI Aayog with focus on agri-based start-ups and ventures working in tech for social good domains. The host institute, Rambhau Mhalgi Prabodhini at AIC-RMP, provides the relevant platform, access, research and a rich experience of over 40 years of working with the NGOs, policy makers, etc. Both these incubators believe in a collaborative approach and share the best practices and learnings with each other due to common sectorial preference and catering to the audience from smaller tier cities.

Recently, in April 2023, PM Narendra Modi laid the foundation stone of Assam Advanced Health Innovation Institute (AAHII) at IIT Guwahati. The AAHII will be a research and innovation institute in the area of medical sciences which includes a 500-bed, connected multi-specialty hospital spread over 12 acres of land in the existing IIT Guwahati campus. The IIT Guwahati and the Assam government have envisioned a medical college where engineers and doctors will work together towards medical innovation, and AAHII is the realization of that dream.

The Assam Startup The Nest is a Government of Assam initiative to create a start-up ecosystem in Assam whereas the IIE is an autonomous institute to undertake training research and consultancy activities in small and micro enterprises focussing on entrepreneurship development. The STINER is a very ambitious, innovative and challenging assignment established and conceived for the people of this region by the Ministry of

Development of North Eastern Region (DoNER). The project's main purpose is to introduce all necessary proven technologies to the inhabitants of the NER, specifically to the community of farmers and craftsmen, in order to improve the quality of their profession through scientific and technological intervention. On 4 June 2018, the Ministry and state government officials mooted for 'Make in Northeast' initiative, as a follow-up to the 'Make in India' initiative inspired by PM Modi.

All in all, to facilitate businesses to stay afloat, incubators will need to step up the handholding of entrepreneurs through enabling support services such as mentorship, pivoting business strategies, alternative funding support, engagement and networking plans, etc. Incubators should continue to work with local administration to help overcome challenges by providing innovative solutions which entrepreneurs can avail.

Table 1

The Status of NER Start-Ups Registered under Startup India[1]

State	2016	2017	2018	2019	2020	2021	2022	Total
Assam	9	34	67	67	119	188	154	638
Manipur	-	4	7	6	12	37	18	84
Tripura	-	-	2	7	23	12	24	68
Nagaland	1	4	2	2	5	7	3	24
Meghalaya	-	-	2	5	-	9	8	24
Arunachal Pradesh	-	-	2	2	-	4	4	12
Mizoram	-	-	2	1	1	2	2	8
Sikkim	-	1	-	2	1	3	1	8
Total	10	43	84	92	161	262	214	866

[1]'The Evolution of North East's Entrepreneurial Ecosystem', *#Startupindia*, https://tinyurl.com/yrzxc9t5. Accessed on 18 September 2023.

Path Forward

Realizing the potential of start-ups and entrepreneurs in the NER requires a multi-pronged approach that includes the following measures:

Educational reforms: Introducing entrepreneurship education at schools and colleges can instil an entrepreneurial mindset from an early age. Skill development programmes should focus on the skills required for modern job markets.

Access to finance: Establishing regional venture capital funds, facilitating tie-ups with national and international investors and simplifying the process of accessing funds are critical steps.

Incubation and mentorship: Setting up incubation centres in urban and semi-urban areas can provide start-ups with the necessary infrastructure, mentorship and networking opportunities.

Policy support: Streamlining administrative processes, offering tax incentives and formulating start-up-friendly policies will encourage more individuals to opt for the entrepreneurial path.

Promoting innovation: Organizing hackathons, innovation challenges and start-up competitions can stimulate creativity and innovation in the region.

Community building: Creating a supportive ecosystem where entrepreneurs can share experiences, collaborate and learn from each other is vital for growth.

Connect with corporates: Encouraging the corporates to set up offices and also giving start-ups access to them so that they can pitch their ideas and solutions can create more opportunity for local start-ups. International conglomerates like Meta and Amazon are eyeing such regions not just to tap the talent but also to get solutions built by start-ups from this region.

Corporate Social Responsibility (CSR) opportunity: There is a huge scope to create livelihood opportunities along with showcasing the outstanding work already being done by self-help groups (SHGs), trusts and non-governmental organization (NGOs) from this region. Hence, the social impact created (and to be created) is massive. There needs to be more CSR funds made available/allotted for beneficiaries such as innovators, start-ups and social entrepreneurs (both not-for-profit and for-profit) which will enable the ecosystem to create the right environment.

The NER of India is at an inflection point where the seeds of entrepreneurship are beginning to germinate. While the challenges are evident, the opportunities are equally promising. Through strategic policy interventions, enhanced education, improved infrastructure and a shift in cultural attitudes, the NER can transform into a vibrant hub of start-ups and innovation. The journey towards nurturing a thriving start-up ecosystem will require collective efforts from governments, educational institutions, industry players and the community at large. As the region awakens to its entrepreneurial potential, it has the chance to rewrite its economic narrative and emerge as a beacon of innovation in India and beyond.

16

THE ENTREPRENEURIAL PUSH

Tage Rita

When I first decided to start my own venture in 2017, leaving behind the security of a well-placed government job in my hometown, it wasn't an easy decision. As a woman from the Northeastern state of Arunachal Pradesh, whose ancestral heritage is predominantly rooted in agriculture, I had a challenging time getting started with my entrepreneurial venture, a winery based out of Ziro valley in the Lower Subansiri district of Arunachal Pradesh. I'm a first-generation entrepreneur and hence, getting adequate mentorship has always remained a struggle. Fortunately, I had my family's support. With my husband by my side, we established our humble winery as a means to create a sustainable market linkage for the locally sourced kiwis of our region, which earlier used to go to waste owing to the lack of an adequate market and cold storage facilities.

If it were three decades earlier, I don't think a woman from my region could have dreamt of running a business, especially in the alcoholic beverage industry, which has been traditionally dominated by men.

Some of the hindrances our people faced back then in taking up entrepreneurship include limited awareness, socio-cultural constraints, limited infrastructure and financial resources, gaps in skills and various regulatory as well as administrative hurdles. But a lot has changed since.

Changing Mindsets and Economic Growth

In the early days, the locals of Arunachal Pradesh relied on traditional means of sustenance, including farming, gathering and hunting. However, with the declaration of statehood, new opportunities have emerged. The government recognized the importance of engaging the local population in governance and began offering them government jobs. Unfortunately, during this initial phase, many people were skeptical about these job prospects, considering them to be scams and inferior to farming. Eventually, individuals did pursue government jobs but shied away from entrepreneurial ventures, primarily due to the perceived risks involved and their lack of a financial background.

Fortunately, the mindset of the new generation in Arunachal Pradesh has undergone a significant transformation. They now embrace both government jobs and entrepreneurship with equal enthusiasm. This change in attitude has had a profound impact on the overall development and economic growth of the state.

In the past decade, the entrepreneurship sector in Arunachal Pradesh and the overall Northeastern region of India has experienced remarkable growth and transformation. These areas, which were previously dependent on agriculture and traditional industries, have now embraced entrepreneurship as a catalyst for economic growth, job creation and innovation.

Over the years, efforts have been made to address the existing challenges and create a more conducive environment for entrepreneurship in Arunachal Pradesh. The government, along with various organizations have introduced policies, skill development programmes and infrastructure development initiatives to overcome these hurdles and promote entrepreneurship in the region. As a result, the entrepreneurship scenario has gradually evolved, providing more opportunities and support for aspiring entrepreneurs.

A Fertile Ground for Entrepreneurship

The Northeast region has always held enormous promise for business operations. However, for a long time, the business environment in the eight states presented significant challenges. Geographic isolation, inadequate infrastructure, financial burdens, limited access to markets, red tape and a generally difficult business climate made it tough to establish and scale a business. Fortunately, in recent years, the government has recognized the need to address these barriers and has made significant efforts to create a more supportive ecosystem for entrepreneurs.

One of the most noticeable enhancements has been the simplification of registration and licensing procedures. Previously, entrepreneurs faced various regulatory roadblocks and time-consuming paperwork that frequently hampered their ability to turn their ideas into profitable enterprises. However, because of the government's efforts, the process is now much easier and efficient. The development of online registration methods and the establishment of dedicated one-stop centres have transformed the way businesses are registered. We can now complete the necessary formalities with ease, saving valuable time and effort that can be channelled towards other critical aspects of our entrepreneurial ventures.

I am particularly proud of the government's focus on women entrepreneurs in Arunachal Pradesh. They understand the potential and importance of women-led businesses in driving economic growth and social empowerment. As a result, they offer special subsidies and incentives to women entrepreneurs, creating a more inclusive and supportive environment for us to thrive.

Furthermore, the government has also addressed the financial challenges faced by entrepreneurs by collaborating with financial institutions to launch schemes and programmes that provide easy access to finance. Collateral-free loans and venture capital funds have become available, alleviating the burden of raising capital and encouraging entrepreneurs to take calculated risks. The

Government of India has launched various initiatives to tackle these challenges. Some examples include the Pradhan Mantri Mudra Yojana (PMMY), Stand-Up India scheme, and Startup India scheme. These programmes provide financial assistance, mentorship and support to entrepreneurs. Additionally, efforts have been made to improve digital literacy and connectivity through the 'Digital North East Vision 2022' initiative.

Ease of Doing Business in Arunachal Pradesh

In Arunachal Pradesh, the government under Chief Minister (CM) Pema Khandu has implemented initiatives like the Micro, Small and Medium Enterprises (MSME) scheme, Deen Dayal Upadhyaya Grameen Kaushalya Yojana (DDU-GKY) and programmes focussed on empowering women entrepreneurs. These efforts have fostered a conducive environment for entrepreneurship in the state. The MSME scheme provides financial assistance, including loans and subsidies to entrepreneurs. The DDU-GKY scheme offers skill development and employment opportunities to rural youth.

Our dynamic leaders such as CM Pema Khandu and Deputy CM Chowna Mein are active advocates in encouraging local entrepreneurs.

Recognizing the state's potential to drive economic growth and uplift the living standards of the people, CM Khandu initiated the Arunachal Pradesh Entrepreneurship Development Programme (APEDP) recently, in a bid to foster an inclusive and thriving entrepreneurial ecosystem in the state. This visionary programme aims to address local challenges and uplift the living standards of the people of Arunachal Pradesh by nurturing aspiring entrepreneurs and equipping them with the resources needed to achieve remarkable success. The APEDP holds the potential to revolutionize the entrepreneurial landscape of the region by inspiring transformation and fostering economic growth.

Additionally, programmes such as the Women Entrepreneurship Development Programme (WEDP), the Women Self Help Group (SHG) scheme and Mahila E-Haat have provided training, credit access, marketing platforms and other forms of support for women-led enterprises. The government has recognized the importance of women's empowerment through SHGs. These groups enable women to come together, pool their resources and engage in income-generating activities. The state government provides financial assistance, training and access to markets for SHGs. Furthermore, the government provides subsidies and financial assistance to women entrepreneurs to encourage their participation in business activities. These subsidies can be in the form of reduced interest rates on loans, tax exemptions or grants for setting up businesses. The Government e Marketplace (GeM) is another platform that facilitates online procurement of goods and services by government departments. It provides a transparent and efficient procurement process, enabling entrepreneurs, including women entrepreneurs, to participate in government tenders and contracts.

Government's Impact on My Entrepreneurial Venture

Personally, for my venture, the introduction of the State Wine Policy in 2015 has enabled me to carry forward my vision and set up a commercial winery in the basement of my home in Hong village, Ziro Valley.

In addition, with the support extended by the Agricultural and Processed Food Products Export Development Authority (APEDA) under the Ministry of Commerce and Industry, we have been able to exhibit internationally in places like Shanghai and Greece, among others. Also, support from the Ministry of Agriculture and North Eastern Development Finance Corporation Ltd (NEDFi) has facilitated our growth.

Over the years, I've also been honoured with various accolades and awards from various private and government institutions. Some of my cherished accomplishments include the prestigious Naari Shakti Puraskar 2021 by the Ministry of Women and Child Development, becoming an alumnus of the 2022 Fortune - U.S. Department of State Global Women's Mentoring Partnership and being able to secure a funding deal at the national platform in Shark Tank India Season 2, among others.

Challenges Faced in Scaling the Winery

It was not easy to connect Ziro Valley with the supply chain. The transporters were not ready to come here and the road conditions were not good, making it difficult to transport the products. It took me two years to complete all the paperwork, registration and other formal procedures. Meeting diverse consumer tastes and demands in the market requires constant innovation and adaptation. We take pride in the fact that our wines can be considered hand-crafted due to the skill and diligence of our team, but the recent pandemic dealt us a heavy blow. Nevertheless, we are determined to bounce back and continue our progress.

Despite the progress made, challenges persist in nurturing and sustaining the entrepreneurship sector. These include inadequate infrastructure, limited access to finance, scarcity of skilled workforce and geographical remoteness. Continued policy support, capacity building and the establishment of an entrepreneurial ecosystem through networking, mentoring and incubation programmes are essential to address these challenges. As much as there is a demand for our wines, the distribution network remains a major challenge. The alcoholic beverage industry can be daunting, with a complicated network.

I believe that the government should create more inclusive policies to foster the growth of start-ups and first-generation entrepreneurs like me. With the right policies and support, we can create a vibrant ecosystem that fosters innovation, growth and job creation. I hope that more and more young people in the state will be encouraged to start their own businesses, driving forward the progress and prosperity of this beautiful region.

Regardless of the obstacles, I am proud of what our organization has become, and I'm grateful for the opportunity to turn my passion into a flourishing business.

Our Winery: Impact and Way Forward

Unlike in metro cities, people in the remote locations of Arunachal Pradesh mostly rely on local produce and tourism to sustain their livelihood. Our winery has helped create a market and a sustainable source of income for the kiwi farmers and others in the community since 2017. The commercial production of our wines has enabled the farming community in Ziro Valley to not only revive the kiwi orchards but to set up their own kiwi nurseries. These nurseries are catering to bulk orders ranging from 5,000 to 20,000 saplings per order.

Additionally, the production of new fruit variants such as pears (with Salyo), plums, peaches and wild apples are further set to strengthen the farming community. The winery offers the respective farmers a ready market to sell their fruits. It is also noteworthy that Salyo plants are on the verge of being revived in the region due to their use in the production of pear wine. Thus, it plays a crucial role in preserving and restoring the ecological balance of the region through replantation of Salyo trees.

Beyond the day-to-day wine production and distribution affairs of the winery, we also welcome guests to our winery tours and sampling of wines. I am hopeful that Northeast India will emerge as a hub for wine tourism, and I look forward to being a part of it.

With a positive outlook and a supportive ecosystem, I am confident that the entrepreneurial landscape in Arunachal

Pradesh and the Northeast region as a whole will continue to thrive and contribute significantly to the region's development and prosperity. I am optimistic about the future of entrepreneurship in our homeland. I encourage our youths, especially aspiring women entrepreneurs to avail the benefits of government initiatives, opt for upskilling and simply follow their hearts and launch their own businesses.

17

DECODING CHANGING VOTING PATTERNS

Pradeep Bhandari

It was five in the morning. I got up early for my exercise as I had a flight to catch in the afternoon. There were meetings lined up in the morning. There were roughly twenty days to go for the Tripura election in 2023. I had an opinion poll scheduled before the elections. I was looking forward to the challenge.

At Tripura

I had travelled extensively in Tripura even in 2018, where we predicted the results of both the opinion and exit poll with 100 per cent accuracy. I remember reporting and analyzing the data. The Left front government was in power, and it had been ruling the state for more than two decades. Public opinion was against the government. Public anger was at its peak. The Bharatiya Janata Party (BJP), banking on Prime Minister (PM) Narendra Modi's aspirational push, created history and defeated the Communist Party of India (Marxist) CPI (M) government. Prime Minister Modi had promised the HIRA (Highways, Internet, Railways, Airways) model of development, the setting up of special economic zones (SEZs) in the state for sectors like food processing and reducing the cost of cultivation of bamboo. The common notion of politicians in India is that they guarantee a lot and make lofty promises, but are poor at execution. However, PM Modi was different. Since his days as the chief minister of Gujarat, I have read stories about his perfect public policy execution and innovative out-of-the-box thinking.

The phone rang. I was told that I was getting late for my flight. Thankfully, I reached the airport on time and boarded the afternoon flight to Agartala.

In my last visit to Tripura for the elections in 2018, I had no option but to reach Agartala via Guwahati. This time around, there was a direct flight from Delhi to Agartala. Prime Minister Modi's promise to the people of Tripura before the 2018 election was implemented on the ground in less than five years. By late afternoon, I landed in the capital city of Tripura. Tripura this time was different, yet similar. The clean and beautiful Agartala airport is a sight I cannot forget. It was a world-class airport with standard infrastructure. The common people were directed systematically by trained staff and signboards. Our local channel partner, *Headlines Tripura,* welcomed us.

Team *Jan ki Baat* was a rage in Tripura. People remembered how in 2018, despite threats from the erstwhile CPI(M) government, we reported the truth and released an accurate survey. I asked Santosh, a local reporter, 'Is the situation still as bad as it was in 2018?' He replied, 'Sir, call me a Bhakt, but with the BJP government in power, gone are the days when we had to fear for our life. Now, we can report what we want, travel anywhere in the state without fear.' During the next few days of my stay, I witnessed the truth myself. The professional protestors who had been running a fake narrative of 'democracy under threat' since 2014, were completely silent. As a reporter, I could feel the right to free speech and the safety of the journalists reinstated after being endangered by the CPI(M) government. My travel to 400 Lok Sabha constituencies made me firmly conclude that if there is one leader who is democratic in a true sense, it is PM Modi.

Unified Payments Interface (UPI) and *Pucca* Houses

The next day, I had to attend Home Minister Amit Shah's rally in Charelam. I reached the rally spot with my team and we sat in the last row. The ground was full, and we were hungry. A local vendor was selling cucumbers. He was completely drained in sweat. I asked him, 'How much is one for?' One packet had three pieces of cucumber in it. He replied gently, '10 rupees.' I offered him a 200 rupees note, but he did not have 'change'. He said, 'You can pay me through UPI,' and took out his scanner. I was pleasantly surprised. My smartphone could access 4G internet, I scanned the code and, within seconds, he received the payment. Nine years ago, no one in the country in their wildest dreams could have imagined that a place in Tripura, 28 km away from Agartala, could become digitally savvy in accepting payments.

India's UPI journey under PM Narendra Modi has been historic. 46 per cent global real time payments originated in India in 2022. The number of UPI transactions increased from 558 crore[1] in April 2022 to 868 crore in March 2023[2]; this is second to no other country in the world. With approximately 120 crore mobile subscribers in India[3], and cost per GB data at just around ₹10, India's digital revolution is a unique global success story. As India has leapfrogged technologically, 140 crore people are standing shoulder to shoulder with PM Narendra Modi. I

---

[1]Jacob, Shine, 'UPI Transactions at Record High in April, Touch Rs 14.07 Trn', *Business Standard*, 1 May 2023, https://tinyurl.com/bdcv85ny. Accessed on 18 September 2023.

[2]'UPI Transactions Surge to a Record High of Rs 14.3 Lakh Crore in May: NPCI', *ABPLive*, 1 June 2023, https://tinyurl.com/2vmerfux. Accessed on 18 September 2023.

[3]'Number of Wireless Subscribers across India between June 2010 and December 2022', *Statista*, 2023, https://tinyurl.com/4ehbwp3u. Accessed on 11 December 2023; The figure for 2022 is 114 crore. This is the number arrived at with the average increase of subscribers over the last year.

returned to Agartala, happy to experience PM Narendra Modi's vision to bring positive changes on ground zero.

The next day, I had to travel to the tribal constituency of Shantirbazar, a traditional CPI(M) bastion. I was stunned to reach Shantirbazar. Even in the interior tribal territories, I could see pucca houses being constructed. I reached one of the houses and asked a lady in her mid-fifties, 'Who is getting your houses made?' The lady whispered, 'Modi.' I further enquired, 'Are you happy? Since when did the construction start?' She opened up with her story and vividly described things to me, 'The construction started six months back. Not just my house. Everyone in the village is getting their houses built under PM Awas Yojana.' To verify, I travelled across the village. Her claims matched the ground reality. Pucca houses were being constructed in the village at a rapid pace. While returning, when I looked out of the window, I could see a similar trend in many other villages.

Prime Minister Modi's welfare statistics are not mere numbers, they are stories of lives that have been transformed by him. When he speaks about more than 119 lakh Awas beneficiaries[4], he comes from a perspective of changing their lives and giving them a dignified existence. My visit to Tripura in 2023 convinced me that the Modi policies have reached ground zero and have impacted lives favourably. We released the opinion poll in February, and after the completion of the psephological exercise, we headed back to Delhi. Thankfully, we could predict the 2023 Tripura election also accurately.

My travel to Tripura, Meghalaya and other Northeastern states gave me an opportunity to gain a first-hand experience of PM Modi's development drives. It is not by luck that the PM Modi-led BJP won all the seats in the Northeastern states in 2019. It was because of his trust-based governance. This is a paradigm shift in the relationship between the state and the people. Earlier, there was

---

[4]See more at: *Ministry of Housing and Urban Affairs*, https://tinyurl.com/2ttbm49h. Accessed on 14 December 2023; This is an evolving figure.

a distrust in the people vis-a-vis the state. Prime Minister Modi put an end to that distrust in 2014. Whether it is the increasing foothold in Assam or the rising from a single-digit vote share to becoming the largest party in Tripura, the BJP under PM Narendra Modi has come a long way in a short period. It was earlier said by commentators that the BJP is a good opposition, but it struggles as a party in governance. These cooked-up narratives have fallen flat when tested on the parameters of truth. The BJP in 2014 won 90 per cent of the seats from 60 per cent of the geography. In 2019, both the vote share and seat share of the party increased substantially. The BJP's pan-India growth post-2014 rests on three pillars:

1) PM Narendra Modi's personal connect with the voter
2) PM Narendra Modi's welfare schemes
3) PM Narendra Modi's ability to motivate the cadre

The Challenge of 2024

In the 2019 elections, the BJP won 14 seats, while its allies secured four, resulting in the National Democratic Alliance (NDA) winning a total of 18 out of the 25 Lok Sabha constituencies in the Northeastern states. The BJP's strongest states in the Northeast are Assam, Tripura and Arunachal Pradesh. The BJP won nine out of 14 seats in Assam. It won both the seats in the states of Arunachal Pradesh and Tripura.

It needs to be underlined here, that while each of the BJP state governments of Assam, Arunachal and Tripura have been exceptional performers, in the Lok Sabha elections, the Modi factor assumes primary significance. The common voter acknowledges that no other Indian PM has worked so hard to improve the conditions in the Northeast. The Modi factor thus will continue to be an important influencer in the 2024 elections. The NDA is likely to retain its 2019 performance in the Northeastern states and possibly even improve its tally marginally in the region.

18

FROM CONFLICT TO PEACE: THE ROLE OF POLITICAL WILL

Rami N. Desai

There was a time when Northeast India was viewed through the lens of not just geographical distance but also psychological distance. Considering the scale of India, the Northeast was considered particularly distant, not so much because it was more distant than other regions but because of a myriad of socio-political and historical issues that had plagued the region. The complexity of the nature of issues and conflicts, the lack of connectivity and infrastructure and the sheer negligence of the impractically carved-out Siliguri Corridor created a conundrum for the experienced researcher, let alone the layman who lived outside the region.

Moreover, the region was conflict-ridden, peppered with active insurgent groups and long-running separatist movements. Each state had multiple insurgencies that collected taxes from the locals—the National Socialist Council of Nagaland-Khaplang (NSCN-K) and National Socialist Council of Nagalim-Isak-Muivah (NSCN-IM) in Nagaland and Manipur, respectively; United Liberation Front of Asom (ULFA) in Assam; and the National Liberation Front of Tripura (NLFT) in Tripura, among many other groups in the same states. Meghalaya in 2013–14 was ranked as the second worst insurgency-affected state in the Northeast in terms of overall fatalities, with Assam accounting for the highest number of fatalities.[1] With an international border of over 5,182 km, with 1,395 km with Tibet in the north, 1,640 km with Myanmar in the east, 1,596 km with Bangladesh in the southwest, the Northeast has always been susceptible to cross-border support for insurgency and infiltration.

The Siliguri corridor, more commonly known as the Chicken's Neck, is a 22-km-wide land mass that creates access to the region for the rest of the country. This corridor—a strategic Achilles heel—is a vulnerable corridor that has been seen as a national security risk ever since it was carved out after Partition of India and the creation of East Pakistan (present-day Bangladesh) in 1947–48. Fortunately, the union of Sikkim with the Indian Republic in 1975 gave India a buffer in the north and somewhat strengthened India's position. However, the ill-imagined carving of the Siliguri Corridor created a psychological divide between what was called the 'Mainland India' and the 'Northeast'.

As a result of this divide, media houses in Delhi rarely covered any developments in the region, despite the frequent instances of violence. I still remember being perplexed by the news coverage of a bomb blast in 2006 that killed four and injured over 40 people at the ISKCON Temple in Imphal, Manipur. The news made it to the national newspapers a few days later, on one of the last pages. The lack of importance of the Northeast in the mainstream consciousness at that time was evident.

This tendency was aggravated by the fact that the region, which comprised eight different states with distinct characters and unique cultures, was seen as a region, not as states. There are over 220 ethnic communities and over 200 dialects in the Northeast. The predominant tribal component and the influence of evangelists on them rendered the understanding of this region far more difficult than any other region in India.

---

[1]'Meghalaya Assessment', *Centre for Development and Peace Studies*, 2014, https://tinyurl.com/mr428j37. Accessed on 18 September 2023.

However, after the change of dispensation in Delhi in 2014, the government led by Prime Minister (PM) Narendra Modi, in a historic move, signed the Naga Peace Accord with the NSCN (IM) in 2015. This agreement took over 80 rounds of talks but immediately brought the region back in focus after decades of isolation. The political will of the government to make the Northeast region a priority was evident. This accord was the first to be signed by the newly elected government; it was followed by many others. From this point onwards, the region began its much-deserved time in the spotlight.

A Complex History of Isolation and Conflicts

I have often thought that, as someone who is not from the Northeast region and a neutral observer, I have a vantage point for assessing the transformation that the region has seen since 2014. I have been travelling the region for more than fifteen years. As a young scholar of the region, I made it a point to live in and travel to the most remote areas in the region—often hotbeds of insurgency, from Changlang and Tirap in Arunachal Pradesh, Haflong in Assam, the hills of Manipur and border areas of Tripura to the length and breadth of the imagined state of Nagalim by the NSCN that led the longest-running separatist movement India had seen.

When I used to travel to the region, many well-wishers would wonder why I was taking a 'risk' by travelling to these areas. Many would say that I'd never grasped the region because I was an 'outsider', a binary often used by those from the Northeast as much as from those from the rest of India. And then there were many whose imagination of tribals and their way of life was staggeringly limited to how Bollywood had presented them to generations of Indians without any fear of repercussion for their lack of research on the subject of their films. They would ask, only half-mockingly, if I would come back alive, wondering if cannibalism was a part of the day-to-day lives of the tribal.

To add to all the warnings that one received before entering the region, once you were there, it was a different world. Despite Guwahati in Assam being the epicentre of all activities, there were hardly any direct flights to other states like Manipur. Roads were hugely problematic, and transportation, therefore, was largely basic. Tourism was abysmal, so one could either hitch a ride or take local buses that were often cramped and dirty. The average network providers were not available, so either you had a BSNL mobile network or one would go to the market to use the STD booth to make occasional calls back home. There were hardly any hotels, and without an option, it was common to stay in the homes of the very generous and hospitable villagers. Even if they just had one bamboo mattress, it would be all yours. However, the thought that would be repeated in my head was, how was it possible that this region had been isolated to such an extent in comparison to the relative comfort we enjoyed in Delhi?

Nevertheless, the vagaries of modern life often bring forth comparisons to age-old complex systems of societies and ideas of comfort, often inaccurately. Such was the case with the Northeast, which was embedded in the British colonial policies of isolation and exclusion that had virtually cut off the region from the mainstream consciousness. In any conversation about the Northeast, it becomes imperative to understand the colonial legacy, recognize the complex nature of issues and truly appreciate the vast distance that has been traversed from being a region ridden with conflict to one of relative peace.

From the Mahabharata to the British

The popular historical narrative of the Northeast region as culturally, religiously and ethnically diverse challenges the collective understanding of India's past. The narrative overlooks the role of the Northeastern population in India's ancient past as well as recent history. For instance, the Idu Mishimi tribe of Arunachal Pradesh trace their lineage to Rukmini, the wife of Krishna. Till date, Idu Rukmini is highly venerated as Inyi Maselo or the Great Mother. The Parashuram Kund in Arunachal Pradesh is also mentioned in the Kalika Purana as the lake where sage Parshurama came to wash his sins away. Hidimba, the wife of Bhima and mother of Ghatotkach in the Mahabharata, were progenitors of the Kachari and Kirat dynasties. Furthermore, while many from the Bodo tribe consider themselves descendants of Brahma and the Karbi tribe descendants of Sugriva. The Manipuri princess Chitrangada married Arjuna; the Naga princess Uloopi fell in love with Arjuna and raised his son Babruvahana. Ancient Indian literature and history are replete with mentions of robust intercultural respect amongst the people and their indigenous ways and evolved acceptance of diversity. However, this narrative was lost with the advent of the British in Northeast India. They were driven by their colonizing agenda and ambition to control the strategically located region. Not only did they diminish the value of the ancient Indian collective civilization but they also created an identity crisis, religious conflict and a psychological sense of distance from the rest of India through their administrative and religious policies.[2]

The period in the Northeast after the British subjugation of the region was highly volatile. The policy of exclusion and exploitation in the Northeast region began almost immediately after the Burmese withdrawal. The British governed from the plains of Assam and made it their seat of power in the Northeast. Though they had previously come into contact with various tribal groups, they failed to understand the distinctions, mindsets, needs and aspirations of the tribal population. On the other hand, the spirit of the independent people of the Northeast did not take kindly to British rule and their agenda of not only exploiting their resources

---

[2]'North-East Tribals and Their Connection to Ancient India', *Sanskriti*, https://tinyurl.com/4sxdtyrd. Accessed on 25 September 2023.

but also restricting their free movement in their own land. The territorial authority imposed by the British was alien to the tribal communities in the region. While a couple of tribal rajas were allowed to stay in power in their remote principalities, the ancient egalitarian political administrative systems were suppressed and replaced by new administrative frameworks, destroying complete social systems that were closely attached to their way of life. The British rulers exploited the vast mineral and natural resources of the region, but they did not pay attention to the economic and social needs of the population, alienating them even further. However, they never lost sight of the value of the untouched resources as well as the importance of a strategically located area in Asia under the direct rule of the British Empire.

It is a fact that the seeds of 'otherness', separate identity and acrimonious relationships with the government were sown during this period of British mishandling of the Northeastern affairs. Due to the negligent attitude towards the tribal by the British, there were rampant raids on British trade routes as well as political uprisings against the authorities. The Lushai-Kuki in Assam raided the British posts as early as 1826. The Aka/Khamti resistances, the Naga resistances, the Sonaram movements, the Kuki rebellion and the Jadonang-Gaidinliu uprising also reflected growing resentment against the British administration and the repressive policies of colonialism.

Exclusion and Regulation

However, to prevent these frequent raids and uprisings by the tribes, the Inner Line Regulation (ILR) was established. At the outset, the reason given for this was to protect the tribes from outside interference. However, the ILR was created to protect British interests from the marauding tribal communities from the hills who used to raid the British subjects, loot and kill. Issued under the Bengal Eastern Frontier Regulation in 1873, it was the first act on the part of the British to segregate the hill tracts of Northeast India from the plains of the valley. The ILR demarcated the limits of the administered areas all along the northern, eastern and south-eastern confines of the Brahmaputra Valley. The British had sought to confine the movement of the tribal communities and limit outside contact with the tribes. To enter the areas beyond the demarcated area for any purpose, a permit would have to be obtained from the deputy commissioner. The ILR finally resulted in the segregation and alienation of the tribes, further causing a massive hindrance to integration with the rest of the nation.

Furthermore, the creation of the 'excluded' and 'partially excluded areas' also added to the alienation of these tribes from the rest of the country. The British policies were narrow-minded. Instead of mitigating the raiding tribes, the tribes became a point of sociological and anthropological fascination for the British. The tribal communities did not receive any benefits, nor were they beneficiaries of any development. The Indian National Congress at the time was extremely critical of the provision for the exclusion and partial exclusion of hilly areas. At its annual session held at Faizpur (1936), the Congress declared:

> This congress is of opinion that the creation of the excluded areas is yet another attempt to divide the people of India in to different groups with unjustifiable and discriminatory treatment and to obstruct the growth of uniform democratic institution in the country. The separation of these areas is intended for the exploitation of the mineral resources and forest wealth in these areas and keep the inhabitants of these areas apart from the rest of India for their easier exploitation and suppression [...] The congress therefore demands the abolition of excluded and partially excluded areas.[3]

---

[3]Pataskar, H.V., *Report of the commission on the Hill Areas of Assam,* 1966, http://tinyurl.com/muas8se2. Accessed on 14 December 2023.

Furthermore, H.V. Pataskar's Report of the Commission on the Hill Areas of Assam (1965–66) stated:

> [The] administration in these areas was confined mainly to maintaining the peace and undertaking sociological studies. Its anxiety was marked by the negative idea of preservation and protection, and we believe, little thought was given to possible ways of stimulating progress. The general outlook was therefore in many ways static rather than dynamic. The administrative machinery was sketchy [...] A kind of distinct barrier was maintained between these hills and the plains during the British rule. Non-tribals were not given admittance to these areas without special permission, which was given rather freely to foreign missionaries. Such restriction deepened the isolation of these areas from the rest of the state.[4]

It is evident that there was considerable opposition to this policy of exclusion. The concern is the irregular distribution of benefits, the future of these excluded areas, the imbalanced development of the Northeast region and the sheer isolation of these tribes from the rest of the nation. Not only was this policy discriminatory but there were questions about the role of the missionaries in the region. Thus, the seed for political development in a regional context was sown during this period.

During this period of debilitating British policies of exclusion and isolation, the only contact that the hill tribes had with the outside world was through Christian missionaries. David Scott, the first Commissioner of Assam, was of the opinion that 'rude tribes were more likely to profit by the teachings of the Gospel.' The then Commissioner of Assam, Major Francis Jenkins, also held the same opinion that 'tribes on the Assam frontier should be brought within the scope of missionary activities as early as

[4]Ibid.

possible as the influence of persons skilled in the languages of these tribes, devoting all their time and attention to humanize these rude races could not fail from being useful to us and to them'.[5]

Moving to Modern Times

The role of British policies and their impact on identity became the genesis of the many conflicts and the prolonged emotional distancing from the mainstream. Today, there has been a 74 per cent reduction in insurgency incidents and an 89 per cent decline in civilian deaths in the Northeastern region in 2021 compared to 2014; over 6,070 cadres of various insurgent groups in the Northeastern states surrendered with over 1,404 arms and joined the mainstream[6].

According to the Ministry of Home Affairs, because of the significant improvement in security in the Northeastern states (see Table 1), Armed Forces (Special Powers) Act (AFSPA) of 1958 was gradually removed from 24 districts and partially from one other district of Assam, 15 police station areas in six districts of Manipur and 15 police station areas in seven districts of Nagaland in 2022. In Arunachal Pradesh, AFSPA has been reduced gradually from 16 police stations and outpost areas bordering Assam to two police station areas in Namsai district, besides Tirap, Changlang and Longding districts. Earlier, AFSPA had been removed completely from Tripura and Meghalaya in 2015 and 2018, respectively.

---

[5]Horam, M., *North East India: A Profile*, Cosmo Publications, 1990.

[6]'Insurgency Incidents in North-East Declined by 74% In 2021: Govt Tells Parliament', *ETV Bharat*, 3 August 2022, http://tinyurl.com/bu65hrrd. Accessed on 12 December 2023.

Table 1

Extremists Killed, Arrested and Surrendered since 1999[7]

Year	Incident	Extremist killed	Extremist arrested	SFs killed	Civilians killed	Extremist surrendered	Arms surrendered	Arms recovered	Persons Kidnapped
1999	1,743	442	1,447	208	599	908	–	355	732
2000	1,963	585	1,536	165	907	1,962	–	574	811
2001	1,335	572	1,456	175	600	797	–	577	399
2002	1,319	571	1,070	142	459	350	177	610	417
2003	1,332	523	1,000	90	494	669	753	442	651
2004	1,234	382	1,099	110	414	1,294	311	481	225
2005	1,332	406	1,498	70	393	555	181	813	239
2006	1,366	395	1,406	76	309	1,430	194	1,008	306
2007	1,491	514	1,837	79	498	524	195	755	292

[7]'Insurgency in North East', *Ministry of Home Affairs*, https://tinyurl.com/2jc2mdmh. Accessed on 18 September 2023.

2008	1,561	640	2,566	46	466	1,112	454	1,164	416
2009	1,297	571	2,162	42	264	1,109	420	1,357	230
2010	773	247	2,213	20	94	846	351	1,057	214
2011	627	114	2,141	32	70	491	381	973	250
2012	1,025	222	2,145	14	97	1,195	612	1,244	329
2013	732	138	1,712	18	107	640	416	1,180	307
2014	824	181	1,934	20	212	291	151	1,104	369
2015	574	149	1,900	46	46	143	69	828	267
2016	484	87	1,202	17	48	267	93	605	168
2017	308	57	995	12	37	130	27	405	102
2018	252	34	804	14	23	161	58	420	117
2019	223	12	936	4	21	158	67	312	108

Consequently, tourism is thriving like never before. Over 1.18 crore domestic and 1.04 lakh foreign tourists visited the Northeastern states of India in 2022[8], from 71.62 lakh in 2014.[9] Further, to enhance regional air connectivity in the region and promote tourism, airports in the North Eastern Region (NER) at Rupsi, Tezu, Tezpur, Pasighat, Jorhat, Lilabari, Shillong, Pakyong, Itanagar and Dimapur involving 64 routes have been operationalized under the Centre's UDAN scheme.

Industry, agriculture and infrastructure have all seen the ripple effect of peace in the region, transforming the Northeast from a stage of obscurity to mainstream consciousness. Recently, it was heartwarming to hear a panellist from the Northeast on a TV debate say, 'there was a time when we were called *chinki*s, we don't hear this anymore.' 'Chinki' is a derogatory term based on the racial perception of Northeasterners being Indo-Mongoloid. With the mainstreaming of the region, such terms and racial divisions, along with the legacy of the colonialists, are quickly disappearing.

Peace Process Initiatives

Many security and political analysts would argue that peace must prevail before development, and others would say development will bring peace and prosperity. However, since 2014, we have seen a successful hybrid model. The government led by PM Narendra Modi brought peace and development together, not allowing one to hold the other hostage. The Northeast, because of its unique history and complex context, has come a long way, and

---

[8]'Tourism in North East India Booms with over 1.19 Crore Domestic and Foreign Tourists in 2022', *#Swarajya*, 28 March 2023, https://tinyurl.com/2edyrt28. Accessed on 18 September 2023.

[9]PTI, 'North East States Saw Steady Rise in Tourist Inflow in 5 Years till FY19: CAG', *Livemint*, 19 March 2021, https://tinyurl.com/3hz646av. Accessed on 18 September 2023.

it has certainly not been an easy task. Conflict in the Northeast has multi-pronged factors that need multi-pronged assessments and solutions—understanding the genesis of conflicts, grasp of ethnic rivalries, historical context, foreign actors, building good relationships with immediate neighbours, bridging trust deficits, acknowledging and celebrating national pride in the Northeast to bridge the psychological divide, as well as creating physical connectivity and infrastructure. Over the last decade, the region has seen major developments in road connectivity, air connectivity, the railway network, waterways, telecom and power, all designed to improve the quality of life of the people. This infrastructure push has been enormously effective, with tangible results.

Alongside the infrastructure push, peace process initiatives were taken towards bringing various long-standing insurgencies and insurgent groups into dialogue with the central government. There were also the signing of many peace accords and agreements of Suspension of Operations (SoO). Starting with the Framework Agreement with National Socialist Council of Nagaland-Isac Muivah (NSCN-IM), the United Liberation Front of Assam (ULFA) (pro-talks) was brought under SoO agreement with the Government of India (GoI) for an indefinite period. Ceasefire agreements are in operation between the GoI and the National Socialist Council of Nagaland/NK (NSCN/NK), National Socialist Council of Nagaland/Reformation (NSCN/R) and National Socialist Council of Nagaland/K-Khango (NSCN/K-Khango). It was decided to extend the ceasefire agreements for another year with effect from 28 April 2023 to 27 April 2024 with NSCN/NK and NSCN/R and from 18 April 2023 to 17 April 2024 with NSCN/K-Khango. These agreements were signed on 6 April 2023. The SoO agreements with the United Peoples' Front (UPF) and Kuki National Organization (KNO) of Manipur have been extended for another year with effect from 1 March 2023 to 29 February 2024. A Cessation of Operation (CoO) Agreement with the Zeliangrong United Front (ZUF) group of Manipur was signed on 27 December

2022, and the ZUF agreed to abjure violence and join the peaceful democratic process as established by the law of the land. Further, the NLFT(SD) Agreement was signed in 2019 and 88 cadres of the NLFT surrendered with 44 arms and the Bru Agreement was signed with representatives of Bru migrants in 2020 for the permanent settlement of Bru (Reang) families in Tripura. A memorandum of settlement (MoS) was signed on 27 January 2020 with Bodo Groups of Assam to solve the long-pending Bodo crisis, which resulted in 1,615 cadres of National Democratic Front of Boroland (NDFB) groups surrendering on 30 January 2020 and disbanding on 9–10 March 2020. An MoS was signed on 4 September 2021 with representatives of Karbi groups to end the decades-old crisis in the Karbi-Anglong area of Assam, which resulted in over 1,000 armed cadres abjuring violence and joining the mainstream society. An MoS was signed on 15 September 2022 with representatives of eight Adivasi groups to end the decades-old crisis of Adivasis and tea garden workers in Assam. This resulted in 1,182 cadres of Adivasi groups joining the mainstream by laying down arms.

Peace processes too come to fruition by understanding the demands in the context of the complex history, culture and identity, with an eye on the near future. To this end, in 2019, the Union Cabinet amended Article 280 and the Sixth Schedule, increasing autonomy and financial powers to autonomous district councils. The amendment also made possible 30 per cent reservation for women in village and municipal councils in Assam, Mizoram and Tripura.[10]

The Ministry of Home Affairs also revised the Surrender-cum-Rehabilitation of insurgents in the Northeast. The revised 2018 scheme allows an immediate grant of four lakhs upon surrender, which is kept in a fixed deposit. It can be accessed as collateral against a loan to be availed for self-employment by

[10]Das, Shaswati, 'Govt EmpowersAutonomous Councils in N-E', *Livemint*, 24 January 2019, https://tinyurl.com/bdhwua8y. Accessed on 18 September 2023.

those who have surrendered. Some of the features of the revised scheme include—payment of a stipend of ₹6,000 per month to each surrendered insurgent for a period of three years, incentives for weapons and ammunition surrendered by the insurgents, vocational training to those surrendered for self-employment and funds for the construction of rehabilitation camps. Further, 90 per cent of the total expenditure incurred on rehabilitation of surrendered insurgents will be reimbursed under security related expenditure (SRE) scheme to Northeastern states.

A concerted initiative was taken to address the historical interstate boundary disputes that were finally resolved. The Assam-Meghalaya boundary dispute dialogue resulted in a memorandum of understanding (MoU). The MoU was signed in New Delhi on 29 March 2022 by the chief minister (CM) of Assam and Meghalaya to resolve the decades-long problem of interstate boundaries of six out of twelve areas of difference. Assam and Arunachal Pradesh have also signed a Declaration on 15 July 2022 at Namsai, Arunachal Pradesh to minimize the border dispute between the two states in respect of 123 villages.

Today, there is no insurgency. Shekhar Gupta, Editor in Chief of *The Print* says, 'There is admittedly that increasingly rare little ambush or clash. You will find more such clashes between armed police and the bad guys in any state of the Hindi heartland than in the entire northeast. Armed banditry is not separatist insurgency.'[11] Shekhar Gupta also attributes this sudden peace in the region to the advent of the new dispensation at the Centre and the 'incredible improvement' in connectivity, such as the many bridges that have been rapidly constructed over the Brahmaputra, facilitating movement across the region.

---

[11]Gupta, Shekhar, 'Northeast a Success Story Not Just for Bjp but All of India. It's All about Getting to End of Bell Curve', *The Print*, 4 March 2023, https://tinyurl.com/3hzsy6sm. Accessed on 18 September 2023.

Concrete Cultural Inclusion

The Northeast region has been a central focus point for the government led by PM Narendra Modi. The Act East Policy is determined to create an environment conducive to the region exploring its full potential and becoming the gateway for India's ambitions of connectivity in Southeast Asia. When data scientist, Rishabh Srivastava and I, tested independent satellite data to see how the region had changed under the United Progressive Alliance (UPA) and National Democratic Alliance (NDA) governments, we found the changes to be remarkable. Satellite images showed that nightlight intensity increased across the region. It grew by 80 per cent in Arunachal in the 2014–18 period (compared to 30 per cent in 2009–13), Manipur by 114 per cent (28 per cent in 2009–13), Assam by 50 per cent (33 per cent in 2009–13), Mizoram by 63 per cent (29 per cent in 2009–13), Nagaland by 59 per cent (15 per cent in 2009–13), Sikkim by 41 per cent (28 per cent in 2009–13) and Tripura by 42 per cent (55 per cent in 2009–13). Government data shows that central government funding for most states in the region increased significantly between 2014–15 and 2018–19.

This has involved not just walking a tightrope in our foreign policy but also keeping an eye on our Neighbourhood First Policy—whether it is a neutral stance towards Myanmar's present dispensation while voicing the importance of democracy or whether it is building on the great relationship with Bangladesh's Sheikh Hasina-led government, that has reciprocated by regularly aiding India by handing over militants.

Finally, the development, infrastructure and peace processes were also strengthened by PM Modi's references in his speeches and his government's focus on reviving forgotten heroes from the Northeast. The nationalism that was once only considered a 'mainland' sentiment was spread through the Northeast by raising the icons of Northeastern tribal and non-tribal communities like

Rani Gaidinliu, Lachit Borphukan, U Tirot Sing Syiem, amongst many others to national status, a much-deserved exercise after being forgotten in the decades after 1947. This played one of the most important roles in creating a psychological connection—a masterstroke to bridge the divide that had deepened over decades of exclusion. Today, the Northeast takes great pride in reviving and putting on a pedestal the great heroes of the freedom struggle for Independence who fought against the British, just like many other Indians from the rest of the country.

In the end, to bring peace to the entire region in the Northeast was never the job of our defence forces. The reality is that, for a complex region dealing with a variety of aspirations and feelings of isolation and otherness that have been forgotten in India's development trajectory, the solutions, just like its problems, needed to encompass the historical, ethnic, colonial and aspirational understanding of the region.

Today, when I travel across the region, I can see the youth returning from the cities they had migrated to, like Bangalore and Delhi, in the quest of better opportunities and security. This reverse migration of original inhabitants is very reassuring. There are big brands and small hotels, like in any other city in the world; roads and highways are safer than ever before, there are no warnings that come my way to reach my destination before nightfall and the media is covering every movement in the Northeast with as much enthusiasm as any other part of the country. The results of a determined political will are evident and traversing from conflict to peace in less than a decade with the PM Modi-led government's multi-pronged initiatives, an example for the world to emulate.

19

ASSAM'S DEMOGRAPHIC CRISIS: TOWARDS A RESOLUTION

Dr Ankita Dutta

On the morning of 15 August 2021, when one of my friends who had then recently joined her new posting at a college in Barpeta district of Lower Assam sent me several pictures from the Independence Day celebrations at her workplace, I was suddenly at a loss of words. Besides a few other districts in Lower Assam, Barpeta too, has been a victim of the demographic change that Assam has been reeling through over the years. The pictures from her college—the 'institutional' celebrations of Independence Day—made me nostalgic and happy at the same time.

The state of Assam has been marred by some of the worst episodes of violence in the recent past. As a child, my father would come home and narrate his election-duty experiences amid calls for poll boycott, re-polling in booths, etc. The dark past that my beautiful state has been a witness to is still unforgettable for us. If 15 August is about enjoyment and celebrations in the rest of India, we, the people of Assam, were compelled to remain confined within the four walls of our homes because of 48-hour bandhs declared by the gun-toting, now-banned, dreaded militant outfit, the United Liberation Front of Asom (ULFA). It was a day of complete boycott of all pro-India activities by every group, organization or institution. In one of the most gruesome massacres carried out by the ULFA in 2004 in Dhemaji district of Upper Assam, a huge bomb explosion during the Independence Day celebrations on 15 August had resulted in the death of 18 people, mostly school children and their parents. The sight of the dead bodies of those little kids was horrific. The ULFA immediately claimed full responsibility for this attack on innocent civilians. It was especially after this brutal incident that the common Assamese people feared stepping out of their homes on both 15 August and 26 January for several years thereafter.

The Congress' Alienation of the Region

Assam is a state that has burned and suffered at the hands of several such unfortunate incidences of dastardly violence time and again, giving further traction to the mainstream media's love for painting the entire Northeast as an 'insurgency-infested state'. However, what went wrong with the ULFA that it suddenly back-tracked on their initial promise of making Assam foreigner-free? The passion, the zeal and the unfathomable energy of the youth who were behind the formation of these organizations had also become part of popular culture, acting as the source of inspiration for many a music composers and lyricists from Assam.

The ULFA was the by-product of a larger political malaise spawned by the attitude of the previous Congress governments at the Centre. The group was very conveniently ignored by a propaganda-peddling academia for a long time. The source of this malaise was rooted in an unexplained sense of anger and discontentment that prevailed since 1962, after Nehru's irresponsible remarks against Assam and its people at the peak of the Indo-China war. In fact, the late Bhupen Hazarika, known as the 'Bard of the Brahmaputra', helplessly expressed the raw sentiments of the people at this hour of crisis through his song *Buku Hom Hom Kore*, whose more familiar Hindi version is *Dil Hoom Hoom Kare*.

The situation became more serious with the Congress Party still toying with various ideas to arrest the restive mood of the Assamese people. The fact that the 'immigrant' Muslim vote-bank was its topmost electoral priority was proven in March 1977, when it was found that there were a total of 560,297 voters in the Mangaldoi Lok Sabha Constituency of Lower Assam, a region bordering Bangladesh. Interestingly, it was one among the few seats that the Janata Party had managed to win back from the Congress (I), which had won 10 out of the total 14 Lok Sabha seats in the state. It was when the sitting Member of Parliament (MP) in the Lok Sabha of the Janata Party passed away a year later that the Election Commission of India (ECI) conducted a bypoll for the Mangaldoi Lok Sabha seat.

Shockingly, within a span of just one year, the total number of electorate in Mangaldoi had increased by a huge 80,000 voters. About 16–17 per cent more people were found to have miraculously appeared almost overnight in the area. It later came to light that the Congress Party, after having lost the seat in 1977, imported nearly 75,000–80,000 Bangladeshi Muslims into Mangaldoi mainly for fattening its electoral coffers.[1] Although there were massive public protests in various parts of the state with many citizens' groups and civil society organizations filing court cases against this dangerous phenomenon, the problem of illegal immigration in Assam was to assume monstrous dimensions henceforth.

Between 2001–2011, the Muslim population in Assam had risen considerably. Six Muslim-dominated districts had increased to nine in 2011.[2] While Badruddin Ajmal's constituency of Dhubri had the largest Muslim population of 80 per cent[3], Barpeta

---

[1]Sethi, Rajat, and Shubhrastha, *The Last Battle of Saraighat: The Story of the BJP's Rise in the North-East.* Penguin Random House India Private Limited, 2017.

[2]Jain, Bharti, 'Muslim Majority Districts in Assam Up', *The Times of India*, 26 August 2015, https://tinyurl.com/3sth6kf4. Accessed on 20 September 2023.

[3]'Dhubri District Religion Data - Hindu/Muslim', *Population Census*, http://tinyurl.com/4cvkn585. Accessed on 14 December 2023.

district showed the highest growth rate of 12 per cent of the Muslims between the two census years. These might sound like politically incorrect concerns or even academically suicidal to talk about, but certain genuine questions need to be asked—are these figures a mere Hindu-Muslim concern or a concern of illegal infiltration from across the border? What about the fear of becoming a foreigner in one's own land that has more to do with culture than religion? There has been a continuous disappearance of non-Muslim ethnic communities from these districts. A case in point would be to understand the demographic transition of Lumding region in undivided Nagaon[4] district. In the Census of 1901, 31 per cent of the district's population consisted of *vanavasi*s, who were largely nature-worshippers, referred to as 'animism' in academic vocabulary. Today, census data barely finds any count of such nature-worshippers in the district. Many of the smaller groups of vanavasis got either wiped out or moved out to other districts, as a result of the increasing pressure exerted on their land and resources by the incoming immigrant population. One of the leading Assamese dailies reported that out of the 144,000 voters in Lumding constituency, only 10,000 were tribal, predominantly belonging to the Dimasa tribe. In fact, the name 'Lumding' itself traces its roots to the Dimasa language. Once the traditional homeland of the Dimasas, Lumding today is chiefly dominated by a non-indigenous population of migrants. The natives were not only stripped of their land rights but have also been rendered economically vulnerable and politically insignificant. Sadly, not a single Dimasa person has represented the constituency till date!

At a time when the issue of Islamic immigration has become an existential danger for the governments in the West and their political paradigms, it would be politically naive to not expect a reaction from the people of Assam.

---

[4]Nagaon is one among the several districts of Assam which has severely borne the brunt of the state's demographic distress.

When, on 5 February 2016, Prime Minister (PM) Narendra Modi was addressing an election rally at Moran in Dibrugarh district of Upper Assam, he came down heavily on the then incumbent Congress government under the leadership of former Chief Minister (CM) Tarun Gogoi. The PM reminded the people of the injustices done to them by the Congress, especially its failure in resolving the immigration problem.[5] As such, the electorate in Assam must have been able to easily relate to this.

Protecting an Ancient Culture

With the coming to power of the Bharatiya Janata Party (BJP) in Assam in May 2016, the common Assamese people began seeing a ray of hope. This was especially evident in Lower Assam, as I have personally visited Nalbari during that time. Nalbari being the birthplace of Himanta Biswa Sarma, the saffron surge was evident everywhere, from the neighbourhood tea stall to the Nalbari college campus. It marked a significant change in the political tide of the state for the first time ever since India's Independence. The political interest of the immigrant Muslims is still primarily represented by the All India United Democratic Front (AIUDF), with the Congress desperately trying to regain its lost space among this group of people. By the Assembly elections of 2016, the demographic composition in a majority of the districts in Lower Assam had changed vastly.

The Assembly Elections of 2021 with CM Himanta Biswa Sarma at the helm of affairs saw the party's continuing bonhomie with the protection of *jaati* (nation), *maati* (land) and *bheti* (home) of the native population of Assam in a far more vocal manner. Chief Minister Sarma was unapologetic in his tone and tenor, more so with respect to his take on the subject of *Miya* poetry

[5]'PM Shri Narendra Modi Address a Public Meeting in Moran, Dibrugarh, Assam : 5.2.2016', *YouTube*, 2016, https://tinyurl.com/ytay9xx9. Accessed on 20 September 2023.

and the assertion of the immigrant Muslim identity that came along with it.[6] Once during his speech at the Agragami Assam event in Guwahati in March 2021, Union Home Minister Amit Shah referred to these elections as a 'battle for preserving the thousands of year old heritage, culture, traditions and ethos' of the ancient land of Pragjyotishpur and Ma Kamakhya.

The gravity of the situation can be understood from the fact that many border areas of Lower Assam and the Barak Valley in Southern Assam are becoming the hotbeds of Islamic fundamentalism, with the Government having busted several jihadi modules associated with Al-Qaeda affiliated terror outfits in Bangladesh over the past few months. Several incriminating facts and evidences of madrasas with deep links to the Ansarullah Bangla Team (ABT) operating in different parts of Assam were unearthed by the Assam Police during the course of investigation.[7] The burgeoning Muslim population in the state provides a larger recruiting ground for Islamists, which eventually poses a serious threat to India's national security.

Both in Lower Assam and the Barak Valley, there is a significant presence of Bangladeshi *maulvi*s and imams who arrive here on tourist visas for 'religious preachings'. However, many a times, these maulvis have openly flouted visa norms trying to indoctrinate the local Muslim youth. Many such maulvis have now been barred by the government from entering the state on the ground of repeated violation of visa norms and regulations. The Government of Assam has adopted a proactive stance to tackle this menace by bulldozing several illegally-constructed

---

[6]Saha, Abhishek, 'Himanta Biswa Stresses Need to Save Assam from 'Miya Poetry, Ajmals', *The Indian Express*, 5 January 2020, https://tinyurl.com/y463rzfb. Accessed on 20 September 2023.

[7]Jaiswal, Umanand, 'Meeting on Assam Madrasas, Police Seek Community Help', *The Telegraph Online*, 5 September 2022, https://tinyurl.com/3pzppkvk. Accessed on 20 September 2023.

madrasas that had been functioning for the past several years.[8]

The Delimitation Exercise and Its Impact

In this context, the delimitation exercise in Assam in early 2023 is expected to benefit both the Assamese and the Bengali Hindus—the earlier inhabitants of the state—in terms of more number of Members of Legislative Assembly (MLAs). However, the biggest beneficiaries of this exercise will be the Bodos and the Karbis, since they will see an additional number of seats in their tally. The temple town seats of Barpeta and Hajo have now been reserved for the Scheduled Castes (SCs) as per the new delimitation template.

As a result of this exercise, the total seats with majority original Assamese population will definitely go up. But it would be wrong to think that this delimitation has been done merely on the basis of the population composition of the different constituencies. Instead, the question of who is 'indigenous' and who is not has been the most important in this regard.

Various other measures taken up by the government, such as mass evictions of illegal settlers from government lands, imposing restrictions on buying land by immigrants, distributing land *pattas* to poor landless *janajati* families, initiating a drive against child marriages, etc., have all been aimed at addressing the rapidly changing demographic scenario of the state through different ways and means. Immediately after CM Sarma assumed charge of office in May 2021, the Assam Cattle Preservation Bill aimed at prohibiting the slaughter of cows and tackling the issue of cross-border cattle smuggling by imposing a complete ban on the transport of cattle outside the state was brought by the government.

---

[8]Chowdhury, Ratnadip, 'Fourth Assam Madrassa Demolished, This Time by Locals', *NDTV*, 6 September 2022, https://tinyurl.com/4rnwrf8s. Accessed on 20 September 2023.

Chief Minister Sarma also announced that government lands all over the state would be freed from encroachment. As of now, hundreds of *bighas* of encroached lands have already been freed in Hojai, Karimganj and Darrang districts. In another significant move at Gorukhuti village in Darrang district, the state government has launched the Gorukhuti Multipurpose Agriculture Project, which was allocated ₹9.60 crore in the 2021–22 Union Budget, in more than 70,000 bighas of government land, huge areas of which had earlier been occupied by illegal immigrants.[9] The government has also allocated funds for the repair and reconstruction works of the *Satras* and the *Namghars*, sites for Vaishnav worship, under the Assam Darshan scheme.

The many measures adopted to protect the local population from illegal migrants have given great popularity to the incumbent BJP government. In this direction, a major success of the BJP in the last five years has been the usage of latest Israeli technology to guard an important stretch of the international riverine border with Bangladesh in Dhubri district of Lower Assam.[10] The same technology is also being used for guarding the vulnerable riverine border in the Barak Valley. Moreover, fencing along the Assam-Bangladesh border is almost complete and the Centre has also undertaken several steps to introduce 'smart fencings' in a few locations. With the hawkish eye of China looming large, it is really praiseworthy that the Northeast has been receiving its due share of attention in the national security framework of the Union Government since 2014.

---

[9]PTI, 'Gorukhuti Eviction Site: Assam Govt Earns Rs 1.51 Crore from Agri Project', *The Print*, 15 March 2023, https://tinyurl.com/3r5jyf6c. Accessed on 20 September 2023.

[10]'Israeli Tethered Drones to Check Cross-Border Crime in Assam's Dhubri District: BSF IG', *The Economic Times*, 5 November 2019, https://tinyurl.com/nhfuaacn. Accessed on 20 September 2023.

20

LACHIT BORPHUKAN: A LEGACY THAT LIVES ON

Nilutpal Gohain

Heroes of a country and the stories of their bravery play a huge role in shaping the cultural identity of a country. The new generations grow up learning from the virtues of such heroes, understanding the legacies that must be upheld and furthered. Respect for the past develops the personalities in the present and resources for the future. One such figure who underlines the virtue of bravery is Lachit Borphukan; his name resonates across the entire length of the mighty Brahmaputra River for every Assamese. The name has been a synonym for bravery in this part of the world since 1671. An average Assamese youth would proudly announce, '*Mur gaat Lachitor tez ase* (I have Lachit's blood running in my veins).'

Mainstreaming Lachit

A couple of years ago, many readers would have asked who is Lachit Borphukan and why his name synonymous with courage. The question should have been answered long ago. However, years of negligence towards the Northeastern region have led to insufficient sharing of knowledge and culture between the eight sister states and the rest of India. Otherwise, Lachit Borphukan would not have remained restricted as a symbol for

Assamese pride. His contribution would have been celebrated across the country as a national reality. His story would have been featured in textbooks and films, telling the world about the greatest generalissimo of the Assamese army who defeated the mighty Mughals in one of the greatest naval battles in the history of India—the Battle of Saraighat. It was a bloody affair, as the Brahmaputra had turned red in the month of March 1671, littered with bodies of Mughal soldiers. A determined Ahom army of mere 20,000 men defeated a swarm of 50,000 warmongers. The Battle of Saraighat changed the attitude, culture and values of the Assamese society.

In 2022, during a first of its kind gathering did the Assam hero find national recognition. Prime Minister (PM) Narendra Modi addressed the closing ceremony of the year-long celebrations of the 400th birth anniversary of Lachit Borphukan in New Delhi, inviting the attention of widespread audience. In line with the PM's vision to honour the unsung heroes of India, PM Modi bowed before the valorous hero who played a pivotal role in preserving the culture of Assam.

'India is celebrating the 400th birth anniversary of Lachit Borphukan at a time when the country is marking "Azadi Ka Amrit Mahotsav", the PM said[1], remembering Veer Lachit's courage and intelligence which glorified not only the history of Assam, but also left a benchmark for the entire country. 'I salute this great tradition on the occasion of the festival of India's eternal culture, eternal valour and eternal existence,' he mentioned, while releasing the book titled *Lachit Borphukan - Assam's Hero who Halted the Mughals*. The PM's words and gestures, standing in the capital of India, raised immense curiosity in the global audience who almost woke up to that part of the history which had earlier been happily ignored.

---

[1]'PM Addresses Closing Ceremony of Year-Long Celebrations of 400th Birth Anniversary of Lachit Borphukan in New Delhi', *Narendra Modi*, 25 November 2022, https://tinyurl.com/4wp9ew8s. Accessed on 20 September 2023.

The Story of Lachit

It was 1664. Assam was reeling under loss after a rapacious and humiliating invasion of the Mughal subahdar Mir Jumla II, one of the trusted but envied commanders of Aurangzeb. The attack exposed the shallowness of some of the Ahom commanders, who took sides with the enemy for petty gains. Internal conflicts were rampant among the nobles, with countrymen fleeing the country and leaving their homes, scared of the tyranny of the conqueror. Swargadeo Jayadhwaj Singha not only had to sign a disgraceful treaty with Mir Jumla, promising him gold, silver and elephants in huge amounts, but also had to part with his beloved daughter Ramani Gabharu, sending her to the Mughal harem. Swargadeo could not survive the embarrassment.

It was amidst anarchy and discord that Swargadeo Chakradhwaj Singha took over the throne. His prime agenda was to free the lost territory as early as possible and for it, he needed a commander who had the authority and popularity to lead an army with high-ranking officials. His first choice was Lachit as his Borphukan—the supreme commander of the armed forces.

Lachit was Momai Tamuli Borbarua's son, the first Borbarua of the Ahom kingdom. He was trained in the Ahom scriptures, Hindu judicatures, economics, kingship, politics, administration and war science from a very young age. He also had the exposure to the happenings of his father's court, which trained him to be an able administrator. Though he was a noble's son, he started off in the humble rank of a 'Ghora Barua', one who tended to the horses. He worked through the ranks of 'Dulia Barbaruah' (the officer who supervised the royal carriages), 'Simaluguria Phukan' (the officer overlooking the Simaluguri fort) and 'Dulakakhoria Baruah' (the officer in charge of the security of the king). Finally, after a few tests, Swargadeo made Lachit the 'Borphukan' of the entire Ahom army.

By the time Lachit Borphukan took over charge as the general, the kingdom was in a sorry state. The army was at its lowest point, and the coffers were almost empty. All the ammunition was lost in the preceding battle. Lachit had a huge task in his hand to build up an adept army and fill up the treasury for a long season of battles. However, Swargadeo was adamant that the attack should happen at the earliest.

However, the chief minister Atan Burhagohain, intervened. He suggested preparing well for the battle rather than jumping into it with inadequate preparation. These wise words worked as a charm, and Swargadeo was convinced that a prepared and planned attack was far better than an unprepared sudden attack. Under the king's personal supervision, Atan Burhagohain and Lachit Borphukan started putting together the army and the kingdom.

After two long years of preparation, on 20 August 1667, the Ahom boats with about 20,000 soldiers sailed towards Guwahati, their western frontier, now the seat of their enemy. The attack on each of the Mughal forts was so sudden and decisive that the Imperial army started abandoning forts without even trying to hold the advancement of the Ahoms. The forts of Kajali, Bahbari and Shah Buruz were captured easily. It was only at the fort of Itakhuli (Guwahati)—the prime seat of the erstwhile Ahom territory, now under the Mughal Thanedar—did the Ahoms face some retaliation. However, it was a short-lived attempt on the part of the Mughals, as it was captured with both wit and might. Within two months of their departure from the capital, the Assamese army not only recovered the lost territories but also their lost prestige and glory.

Aurangzeb wanted to teach a lesson to the Ahoms and decided to counter-attack. He chose Raja Ram Singh to be the commander of the imperial army, which comprised 30,000 infantry, 18,000 export Turkish cavalry and 15,000 archers. Borphukan knew it would be impossible to defeat the huge army in the open plains. In February 1669, Ram Singh arrived at the frontiers of Ahom kingdom. The Ahoms, on their end, had started building impregnable walls and mud embankments in and around Guwahati to halt the movement of the Mughal army, particularly the cavalry. The only way of entering the city was through the river, which was the Mughal army's weakest point, since they did not have naval preparedness. However, concerns were piling up. The Ahoms underestimated the size of the enemy, and the need to erect a few more ramparts and embankments arose. The only way they could buy some time was to open insincere negotiations with the Mughals. It was also a calculated war strategy, for the Mughals were finding it hard to deal with the geographical conditions. The climate of the Brahmaputra Valley was harsh for the Mughals. Many perished with pestilential diseases. Their provisions also exhausted and the long flood season cut off their routes of supplies.

Inspiring and interesting is the story that followed since the huge loss of the Ahoms in the battle at Alaboi Hills. Ram Singh and his troops were motivated to launch the decisive attack. Lachit Borphukan was then seriously ill. The Ahom troops became aimless and timid with the absence of their commander general. They started to prepare the boats to leave Guwahati and sail upstream abandoning the battlefield. The Mughals kept advancing towards Guwahati. Lachit grabbed his sword and ran down to his boat, pushing four of the sentries into the water. A rumour spread like wildfire that the Borphukan was drowning all who were running away from the battlefield.

Lachit took his boat right in front of the Mughal flotilla and started attacking them with cannons and muskets. Looking at his bravery, other Ahom war boats returned and sailed towards Lachit, joining him in attacking the Mughals. The musketeers and archers who were still at the banks also attacked the Mughal boats. Mughals could not advance further and they decided to hold their position.

However, soon Lachit realized that their valour would go in vain as the ammunition present on the boats would soon be exhausted. He ordered the boats to line up into a straight line, joining one boat to the other, making a bridge over the river. That way, supply of ammunition among the boats as well as from the banks continued while the Mughals soon lost their ammunition. As a result, the Mughals had to retreat after losing most of their men.

During those days, Guwahati and the area around it was called Saraighat, and hence the battle came to be known as the Battle of Saraighat. Lachit Borphukan died soon after the war and he was laid to rest at Jorhat. A 35-feet-high statue of Lachit has been installed in the middle of Brahmaputra River in Guwahati as a mark of respect to the great soul.

Prime Minister Modi's Words

In the 1,000-year-old history of human existence, PM Narendra Modi remarked—there were numerous civilizations that walked the earth, many that seemed imperishable, but it was the wheel of time that brought them down to their knees.[2] India, as a country, faced unexpected adversities in history, and withstanding the unimaginable terror of foreign invaders, has still stood immortal with energy, consciousness and integrity. He pointed out that whenever there was a crisis in any part of the country, some personality emerged to take responsibility and fight back—be it Birsa Munda in Jharkhand or Chhatrapati Shivaji in Maharashtra. In each epoch, saints and scholars came to protect the spiritual and cultural identity of India. Brave hearts like Lachit Borphukan proved that forces of fanaticism and terror perish eventually but the immortal light of Indian life remains eternal. The PM's emphasis has led to a lot of interest in the national media and academia, not only in Lachit but also in comparing the history of the state vis-a-via the rest of India.

---

[2]Ibid.

The PM reiterated in his speech, that India wants to scrap the mentality of slavery and take pride in its heritage. While celebrating its cultural diversity, the country is trying to look back at its own provinces to acknowledge the change-makers from its history. 'Immortal sons of Maa Bharati like Lachit Borphukan are the inspiration of fulfilling the resolutions of the Amrit Kaal. They make us familiar with the identity and glory of our history and also spur us to dedicate ourselves to the nation,' the PM added. In the story of Lachit, what comes out significantly is the fearlessness, intelligence and fighting spirit of a leader who stood up for the dignity of his land and its people.

Prime Minister Modi complimented the Assam Government led by Himanta Biswa Sarma for taking steps to celebrate the legacy of its hero through the three-day programme in the national capital to celebrate the four-hundredth birth anniversary of the seventeenth century Ahom general. The PM further mentioned that very soon, projects like a museum and a memorial in Assam would be initiated because such steps will help the younger generation to know the history of sacrifice and bravery. 'Lachit Borphukan's life inspires us to live the mantra of "Nation First". His life inspires us to rise above self and to give the highest priority to the national interest. His life teaches us that instead of nepotism and dynasty, the country should be supreme,' he said. Taking instances from the life of Veer Lachit Borphukan, the PM said, 'no person or relation is above nation.' Connecting the region with the country, he insisted that, when a nation knows its real past, only then it can learn from its experiences and tread the correct direction for its future. Unlike the earlier governments that shut their eyes towards India's Northeast, the PM encouraged the new age learners to look at India's past with an open mind. 'It is our responsibility that our sense of history is not confined to a few decades and centuries,' he explained.

Honouring the Hero

On 24 November, the state celebrates Lachit Divas every year to commemorate Veer Lachit Borphukan's birth anniversary. However, 24 November 2022 was different. It was the 400th birth anniversary of the war hero and Chief Minister (CM) of Assam, Himanta Biswa Sarma left no stone unturned to mark the celebrations in a grand way. The three-day-long celebrations at Vigyan Bhawan, New Delhi, had panel discussions, deliberations and plays about Lachit Borphukan and his accomplishments. A wonderful display of artefacts belonging to the Ahom era, rare manuscripts and ancient texts were also showcased for the visitors and guests. Minister of Home affairs Amit Shah was present on the occasion to release a documentary on Lachit Borphukan produced by *History TV18*. The hour-long docudrama covered all aspects of the General's life. Assamese people were filled with pride when the documentary was released all over the country across major satellite channels. It was a commendable step by the state government to present Lachit Borphukan nationwide on a large scale. The year-long programme covered by various media agencies in multiple formats helped spread the word far and wide, while raising awareness among the audience beyond Assam.

The then president Ram Nath Kovind had kickstarted the celebrations for the 400th birth anniversary of Lachit Borphukan and laid the foundation for a war memorial along with a 150-foot bronze statue of the commander. Chief Minister Sarma had written to his chief ministerial counterparts, requesting them to include a chapter on Lachit Borphukan in the school and college curriculum of their respective states. The PM further suggested creating a grand theatre play on Lachit Borphukan on the lines of the one on Chhatrapati Shivaji Maharaj, and taking that to every corner of the country, thereby boosting the resolution of Ek Bharat, Shreshtha Bharat. 'We have to make India developed and make Northeast, the hub of India's growth. I am sure that the spirit of 400th Jayanti of Veer Lachit Borphukan will give strength to our resolve and the nation will achieve its goals,' the PM concluded his speech.[3]

The role of a bureaucrat in a government machinery is immense, but the kind of leadership one works under is equally important. I, being a bureaucrat myself, can say that the current government under the dynamic leadership of CM Sarma has inculcated the values of Lachit Borphukan and the path shown by him to achieve unachievable feats. The governance has gained such a momentum that our beloved state will soon emerge as one of the best performing states in the country in every sector of economy and welfare.

Lachit Borphukan and his legacy have stayed with the Assamese society since the Battle of Saraighat and it will continue to inspire young minds with a sense of patriotism for their state. But it was only after 400 years and with a collaborative effort of the current governments, both at the Centre and the state, that his valour and sacrifice will motivate the future generations of the entire country. Now, he is a national hero.

---

[3]Ibid.

21

TRANSFORMING MEGHALAYA'S HEALTHCARE SYSTEM

Alexander Laloo Hek

I joined the Bharatiya Janata Party (BJP) way back in 1996 inspired by the vision of the then nation leaders of the party, our former Prime Minister (PM) Late Shri Atal Bihari Vajpayee and Shri Lal Krishna Advani. I was perhaps one of the BJP's earliest members from the Northeast. My sole inspiration and attraction towards joining the BJP was that, it was a national party with a clear long-term mission and vision of working for the country's interests. The BJP and its leaders have been sincerely working hard to make our country corruption free. As an Indian, I have full faith in the BJP and also believe that the party will keep on developing our Northeastern states to strengthen the country.

In 1998, when I was the President of Bharatiya Janata Yuva Morcha (BJYM) Meghalaya state, I first met PM Narendra Modi. Back then, he was the national secretary in charge of the National BJYM. We had a long meeting and conversation about strengthening of the party organization during the all-India office bearers meeting of National BJYM organized by Meghalaya BJYM, which was held in my constituency at Pynthorumkhrah, Shillong.

In 2014, Modiji, then chief minister (CM) of Gujarat, personally invited me to Ahmedabad when I was the minister of health and family welfare for Meghalaya. He had offered that I should contest the Lok Sabha seat from Shillong on a BJP ticket. However, due to some unavoidable circumstances of mine, I could not accept the offer. I extended all my cooperation and introduced him to a retired bureaucrat and a senior reputed politician from our state so that our discussion could be furthered.

Modiji is a great planner, positive thinker and far-sighted personality. Since my long innings in the politics of our beloved country, I have seldom experienced a PM who can be so down to earth and hard-working. He never wastes his time and always ensures the best services to the people of the nation. He is a decision-maker who always thinks about the country's long-term interests before anything else.

In recent years, I got two significant opportunities to work closely on Modiji's vision. These were during my tenure as health and family affairs minister of Meghalaya. The first opportunity was in implementing the Ayushman Bharat Digital Mission (ABDM) in Meghalaya, with the aim to develop the backbone for an integrated health infrastructure. The second was during our fight against the Covid-19 pandemic. On both occasions, I learnt immensely from the scale of planning that goes into Modiji's policies.

As Health Minister

During my tenure as the health minister of Meghalaya, I found Modiji to be extremely diligent about ensuring that the healthcare provisions reach the grassroots. A large population of India is remotely placed. Neglecting them would have caused havoc. With this clarity, he monitored the provision of the best healthcare percolating to the poorest sections of our society. I worked closely with the central government in successfully implementing the Ayushman Bharat under the Pradhan Mantri Jan Arogya Yojana (PM-JAY), which is named Megha Health Insurance Scheme (MHIS). The objective was to increase awareness about Ayushman Bharat and reach out to the beneficiaries with information about availing the services. The thematic approach essentially covered both the pillars of Ayushman Bharat schemes i.e., the PM-JAY as well as the Pradhan Mantri Health & Wellness Centres (HWCs). These health centres were created in February 2018, when the Government of India (GoI) announced that 150,000 (HWCs) would be created by transforming the existing Sub Centres and Primary Health Centres to deliver comprehensive primary healthcare and declared this as one of the two components of Ayushman Bharat.[1]

In the Financial Year (FY) 2021–22, the total number of footfall in Ayushman Bharat Health and Wellness Centres (AB-HWCs) was 1,149,642 and in FY 2022–23, it was 1,605,134. This shows an increase of 5 per cent in footfall in all the operational HWCs as compared to the last two years. For the FY 2023–24 from April–June, the total footfall is 508,867 in these HWCs.[2]

Till the FY 2022–23, the State of Meghalaya has scaled up the implementation of Comprehensive Primary Health Care Programme in all 11 districts of the state with a total of 593 AB-HWCs, 114 CHC (Community Health Centres), 460 PHC (Primary Health Centres) and 19 UPHC (Urban Primary Health Centres) to be made operational as AB-HWCs. The state under the National Health Mission (NHM) has also created a cadre of mid-level health providers (MLHPs) through a six-month certificate course in community health. These MLHPs are being posted at the sub-Health Centres. Till date, a total of 380 MLHPs have been posted in HWCs. In Meghalaya, the AB-HWCs programme was implemented in 2018 and till date, the state has been able to operationalize 448 AB-HWCs.[3] Under the Pradhan Mantri

---

[1]'About Pradhan Mantri Jan Arogya Yojana (PM-JAY)', *National Health Authority*, https://tinyurl.com/yeywkk4b. Accessed on 20 September 2023.

[2]All figures for which no separate source has been provided have been obtained from sources privy to the minister's office.

[3]'Meghalaya Bags Award for Achieving 448 Health and Wellness Centres', *Government of Meghalaya*, December 2022, https://tinyurl.com/33p4wmy6. Accessed on 25 September 2023.

Ayushman Bharat Health Infrastructure Mission (PM-ABHIM), 75 sub-Health and Wellness Centres are under construction by the village health councils in all the districts in the state. These sub-Health Centres will also function as HWCs.

Battling Covid-19

Meghalaya faced one of its toughest challenges during the Covid-19 pandemic. In a hilly state, combating a pandemic is always tough. However, it was made easy by the constant support, direction and hand-holding from the central government. Here again, PM Modi led the nation's fight against the pandemic by example, inspiring others like me to work harder.

During the Covid-19 pandemic in Meghalaya, the central government announced the Pradhan Mantri Garib Kalyan Yojana/Package (PMGKP) to help the poor. This package, along with other objectives, aimed to prevent disruption in the employment of low wage earning employees. At the same time, the Government of Meghalaya has partnered with the United States Agency for International Development (USAID) to launch mobile vaccination initiatives to administer vaccines for the underserved and marginalized communities who have limited access to vaccination centres and live in far-flung areas.

Table 1

Data for Total Vaccination, Meghalaya June, 2023

Dose 1	1,446,927
Dose 2	1,087,797
Precaution Dose	91,034
Total Doses	2,625,758

In Meghalaya, the BJP is part of the ruling coalition led by CM Conrad Sangma. I am the sole BJP minister in the Meghalaya

Cabinet, in charge of animal husbandry and fisheries. However, in the years to come, under PM Modi's vision and guidance, we hope to emerge as the ruling party in Meghalaya.

Meghalaya still has immense untapped potential and a lot of scope for improvement, particularly in the areas of health tourism, rural connectivity and entrepreneurship. Some of the key points on our manifesto for Meghalaya include promoting better tourism and wellness through the local tribal therapy and medicine, creating more awareness for generating entrepreneurship in our state and bettering road connectivity in villages. Under PM Modi's continued guidance, Meghalaya too can realize its full potential.

22

A RESURGENT TRIPURA

Dibakar Dutta

The last nine years of the Modi government have ushered a new era of development for Northeast India, especially my native state of Tripura.

For several decades, the progress of Tripura had been marred due to poor connectivity, geographical isolation, under-utilization of resources, shutting down of industries, limited infrastructure development, 25-year-long communist misrule and indifference of Union governments. When Prime Minister (PM) Narendra Modi came to power in 2014, he took up the cause of Northeast India's development on a mission mode. Tripura was one of the biggest beneficiaries of his vision, where he advocated the HIRA (Highways, Internet, Railways and Airways) model of development.

When the Bharatiya Janata Party (BJP) was elected to power in the state in 2018, the double-engine government made a massive difference in the lives of ordinary residents of Tripura.

Highways

One of the key highlights of Tripura's success story has been the increased focus on the development of highways and inter-state connectivity. The objective behind it is to increase connectivity to industrial clusters and enhance logistical efficiency and freight movement. In October 2020, the Union Minister of Road Transport and Highways, Nitin Gadkari, laid the foundation stone for nine national highway projects in Tripura. With a budget of 2,752 crore, the projects covered a distance of 262 km and provided a hassle-free inter-state travel as well as international travel to Bangladesh. The projects benefited the towns of Jolaibari, Belonia, Kailashahar, Khowai, Kumarghat, Manu, Churaibari and Agartala.[1] They have ensured safe and fast movement to historic, religious and tourist places in the entire state. At the same time, these projects have generated employment opportunities, improved the transport of agricultural goods and ensured speedy access to emergency and healthcare services.

The Centre also sanctioned an amount of ₹456 crore in February 2022 for the upgradation of the Lalchara–Kanchanpur section of the National Highway (NH) 44A under the Bharatmala Pariyojana.[2] In December of that year, PM Modi inaugurated a project to widen NH 8. He also laid the foundation stone for 32 road projects under the Pradhan Mantri Gram Sadak Yojana (PMGSY). The PM also launched a total of 112 road projects and district highways of 542 km.

In June 2023, it was recommended by the PM Gati Shakti national master plan that a 135 km stretch of the Khowai-Teliamura-Harina highway be widened into two lanes at a cost of 2,486 crore.[3]

---

[1]Nag, Devanjana, 'Big Infra Upgrade in Tripura: North Eastern State to Get Nine National Highway Projects! Details', *Financial Express*, 27 October 2020, https://tinyurl.com/mtzjzbmp. Accessed on 20 September 2023.

[2]Ali, Syed Sajjad, 'Centre Sanctions ₹456 cr. For Highway Stretch in Tripura', *The Hindu*, 16 February 2022, https://tinyurl.com/ycye2jjh. Accessed on 20 September 2023.

[3]Das, Arun Kumar, 'How Rs 2,486 Crore Road Widening Project in Tripura Will Improve Connectivity and Industrial Activity', *#Swarajya*, 10 June 2023, https://tinyurl.com/y8dwaf3w. Accessed on 20 September 2023.

It must be mentioned that in the past nine years, NHs in the state have increased from one to six. While acknowledging the states's development, PM Modi has also said that Tripura is on the path of becoming a 'trade gateway and logistics hub' of Northeast India.[4]

Internet Connectivity

One of the stark differences that I witnessed during my recent trip to Tripura was the high-speed internet and its easy access at affordable prices. With the entry of private players now, besides the state-run BSNL services, internet penetration in Tripura has increased by several folds.[5] Chief Minister (CM) Manik Saha has also attested to this fact and said that Tripura now has the third-highest high-speed internet in the entire country.[6] This has brought about positive changes in the people's way of life. Due to the availability of high-speed internet services, residents of Tripura have seamlessly adopted e-payment systems and decreased their reliance on cash. I spotted QR codes at every shop, and even vegetable vendors had actively adopted to the digital way of life.

Perhaps, the biggest benefactors of high-speed internet in Tripura were the young men and women from the state, who work in the service sector in metropolitan cities. During the pandemic, they could return to Tripura and work from the comfort of their homes without worrying about their internet connectivity. Such a scenario was unimaginable a decade ago.

---

[4]Deb, Debraj, 'Tripura Becoming Trade Gateway, Logistics Hub of NE: PM Modi', *The Indian Express*, 19 December 2022, https://tinyurl.com/338vtpre. Accessed on 20 September 2023.

[5]Hussain, Afrida, '108 Remote Villages in Tripura Get Internet', *India Today*, 14 January 2023, https://tinyurl.com/2uemmh5t. Accessed on 20 September 2023.

[6]'Tripura Has Third-Highest High-Speed Internet Connectivity in Country: CM Manik Saha', *ANI*, 12 June 2023, https://tinyurl.com/nkpta6v9. Accessed on 20 September 2023.

Railways and Airways

For the most part of its history, Tripura had only metre-gauge railway tracks. As such, residents of the state had to travel to Assam to board trains such as Shatabdi and Rajdhani Express. It was the only way one could travel to far-off destinations such as Delhi, Kolkata, Chennai and Bengaluru via train from Tripura. I distinctly remember travelling to Guwahati from Dharmanagar on a metre-gauge train and then changing to a broad gauge track to board a train to Chennai in 2001. A similar scene unfolded during my trip to Delhi from Tripura for my undergraduate admission in June 2014.

All of this changed in January 2016 when the first trial broad gauge train entered Agartala.[7] A year later in October 2017, the much-awaited Tripura Rajdhani Express was flagged off to Delhi.[8] As a result, travel time from all parts of the state to the capital city has been significantly reduced due to high-speed trains plying on broad gauge.

We now have superfast long-distance trains that take us to far-flung destinations, without the need to travel to Assam first. The progress in this sector has been remarkable. What we did not achieve in several decades was made possible within a span of a few years, starting in 2014. Improvements are being constantly made even now to ensure hassle-free travel for the residents of Tripura. For instance, in February 2021, the Agartala-bound Rajdhani Express received a facelift with upgraded facilities.[9]

One of the promises made by PM Narendra Modi to the people of Tripura was the development of airways. In January

---

[7]'Broad Gauge Reaches Tripura', *Railway Gazette International*, 14 January 2016, https://tinyurl.com/mr4957fw. Accessed on 20 September 2023.

[8]'Tripura Rajdhani Express to New Delhi Chugs off from Agartala', *The Statesman*, 28 October 2017, https://tinyurl.com/bd7kf33v. Accessed on 20 September 2023.

[9]'Tripura: Agartala Bound Rajdhani Express Upgraded for Better Travel Experience', *Northeast Now*, 13 February 2021, https://tinyurl.com/3uwyhtrd. Accessed on 20 September 2023.

2022, he inaugurated a new integrated terminal building of the Maharaja Bir Bikram (MBB) Airport, which is equipped with state-of-the-art facilities. The terminal, which is built at a cost of ₹450 crore, can handle between 2,000–2,500 passengers at a time.[10]

In April 2023, the second-largest air cargo terminal in the Northeast was inaugurated at the MBB airport.[11] Meanwhile, efforts are underway to introduce international flight services from Agartala.[12] The Ministry of Civil Aviation has also proposed building a second airport in the Unakoti district of the state to improve air connectivity and promote tourism.[13]

Infrastructure Development and Direct Benefit Transfer

Besides the construction of highways, a special emphasis has been laid on infrastructure development by the government in Tripura. For instance, a memorandum of understanding (MoU) was signed between the Tripura government and the National Highways Logistics Management Limited (NHLML) for the development of four ropeways in the Northeastern state.[14]

---

[10]Bose, Joydeep, 'PM Modi to Launch State-Of-The-Art Airport Terminal in Tripura Today. All You Need to Know', *Hindustan Times*, 4 January 2022, https://tinyurl.com/4n4x5m67. Accessed on 20 September 2023.

[11]PTI, 'Northeast's Second Largest Air Cargo Terminal Opened in Tripura's Agartala', *Business Standard*, 28 April 2023, https://tinyurl.com/442pa4nv. Accessed on 20 September 2023.

[12]PTI, 'Tripura CM Meets Scindia, Demands MBB Airport Be Declared International', *The Print*, 24 April 2023, https://tinyurl.com/yptk2jbf. Accessed on 20 September 2023.

[13]'Greenfield Airport to Come Up in Unakoti District of Tripura', *The Hindu*, 14 January 2023, https://tinyurl.com/yy88dzy5. Accessed on 20 September 2023.

[14]Nath, Abhijit, 'Seven New Projects Worth over Rs 10,000 Crore Announced for Tripura; CM Expresses Gratitude toward PM Modi', *Northeast Today*, 11 November 2022, https://tinyurl.com/2dstasxt. Accessed on 20 September 2023.

In October 2022, the foundation stone of the Tripura National Law University was laid at Narsingarh, beside the Maharaja Birendra Kishore Manikya Museum and Cultural Centre in Agartala. A month later, CM Manik Saha inaugurated the Tripura Film and Television Institute (TFTI) in Agartala. In December 2022, PM Narendra Modi inaugurated the state's first dental college.

Recently, the state government has launched the 'Tripura Energy Vision 2030 Road Map' with the aim to generate about 500 MW of solar power by 2030. Tripura has also identified more than 2,000 acres of land for public-private partnership, industrial development, special economic zones (SEZs) and sector-specific projects with support from the Modi government at the Centre.[15]

According to Uttar Pradesh CM Yogi Adityanath, three lakh families in Tripura have received houses under the Pradhan Mantri Awas Yojana (PMAJ) while 2.70 lakh people benefitted from the Pradhan Mantri Ujjwala Yojana (PMUY) scheme. He also informed that about 2.5 lakh farmers in the state have been the beneficiaries of the PM Krishak Sanman Nidhi welfare scheme.[16]

Increased Remuneration for Employees

One of the long-standing demands of Tripura government employees was the revision of their pay structure. As recently as 2017, state government employees (mostly teachers) were being paid in accordance with the Fourth Pay Commission (prevalent in the late 1980s). There was also a demand to align the dearness allowance (DA) with that of central government employees. When

---

[15]Deb, Debraj, '9 Years of Modi Govt: Tripura CM Saha Says Northeast Undergoing Massive Development', *The Indian Express*, 29 May 2023, https://tinyurl.com/ytuxtaba. Accessed on 20 September 2023.

[16]'BJP-Ruled Tripura Got Development at Speed of Bullet Train: Yogi at Poll Rally', *The Print*, 8 February 2023, https://tinyurl.com/5cep52jc. Accessed on 20 September 2023.

the BJP government came to power in 2018, it announced a hike in the pay scale of employees and pensioners at par with the Seventh Pay Commission.

After years of remaining underpaid under the Left regime, the employees finally had their due. As promised, the Tripura government revised the DA, first with a three per cent hike (February 2021)[17], then a five per cent hike (August 2022)[18], followed by a whopping 12 per cent hike (December 2022)[19].

Waking Up to Progress

Life in Tripura has always been slow and laid back. But the contagious spirit of 'Atmanirbhar Bharat' has begun to change the attitude of the residents of the state. The *'cholbe, cholche'* sense of complacency is now under challenge. People are actively giving up the laidback attitude and joining the mainstream with zeal and fervour.

The entrepreneurial spirit of creating one's own destiny was visible during my recent trip to Tripura; it had overpowered our traditional way of resigning to our fate. This newfound attitude of self-reliance did not develop in a day. It is a manifestation of the progress and development that we have witnessed in the past nine years in Tripura, first under the Modi government at the Centre and then under the BJP state government.

Tripura is no longer a state whose geographical location could only be expressed in terms of its proximity to Assam. We

---

[17]PTI, 'Tripura Government Announces 3% Hike in DA for Employees from March', *The Economic Times*, 26 February 2021, https://tinyurl.com/mrajusac. Accessed on 6 December 2023.

[18]'Tripura Hikes DA for State Govt Employees by 5% Ahead of Assembly Polls in 2023', *Livemint*, 3 August 2022, https://tinyurl.com/2kvzhjmm. Accessed on 6 December 2023.

[19]PTI, 'Tripura Declares 12 per Cent Hike in DA for Government Employees', *The Economic Times*, 27 December 2022, https://tinyurl.com/4sa6mfbd. Accessed on 20 September 2023.

have not only grown by leaps and bounds but have been able to showcase our unique identity, culture and success story to the rest of the country.

23

DECODING MANIPUR'S ENTREPRENEURIAL JOURNEY

Lairenjam Niranjan Singh

Manipur, a scenic state nestled in the Northeastern part of India, is often praised for its natural beauty and rich culture. However, it has faced its share of challenges, including economic stagnation, insurgency and unemployment. In recent years, the entrepreneurial spirit in Manipur has been on the rise, and the success story of my skill-training venture is a testament to the potential and the growth of the start-up ecosystem in the region.

From Adversity to Opportunity

Having grown up in insurgency hit Manipur in the 1980s and 90s, my parents were always wary about our education and the environment in which we were growing up. General infrastructure in the state was poor and the education was often disrupted due to the fear psychosis instilled by the insurgent groups. Therefore, we were sent away to boarding schools to get schooling in a peaceful environment. However, when we used to come to Manipur for summer and winter vacations, on our way home from the airport, I always saw the same dilapidated buildings and potholed roads for almost 15–20 years! As a child, I remember, I often asked my parents—when will 'my Manipur' ever develop and be peaceful? My father, who used to serve the Government as an Indian Police Service (IPS) officer, must have probably engaged his whole professional life dealing with insurgency in Manipur. While engaging with youth and social organizations, he often mentioned that the solution for Manipur's problems lie in economic development. If I meander back those old days through my mind, I can visualize the real scene of underdevelopment, unemployment among youth, lack of livelihood and the subsequent insurgency movements. All these years, from mid-80s till early 2010, I was away from Manipur for education and worked in different parts of the world. Unfortunately, I lost my dear father to the savagery of insurgency in the year 2004. However, his life marked with dealing the complex nature of insurgency and his desire for rapid economic development in Manipur, made me contemplate the need to do something meaningful and impactful for the society.

Since I had special interest in training while I was working in the corporates, I decided to start a skill-training company which is inspired by my father and is named after him. My organization is a regionally focussed training company in Northeast India. The whole idea behind it was an innate desire to engage the youth of Manipur and pull them away from the trap of social unrest, unemployment and insurgency to channelize their energy to earn a livelihood for the family. We strongly believed that Northeast India's development could fully happen when its human resource is effectively developed. We started operations in 2013 in Imphal, Manipur. Those days, the start-up ecosystem was not evolved as much as it is today. There were no angel funds and venture capital funds. The initial days were bootstrapped from personal finances, family help and operating revenues of the company.

Bold Policy Change in 2015

Back in 2013, skill-training was conducted by the labour department of state governments by the Skill Development

Initiative (SDI) scheme. Labour department has always been considered a minor department with undermanned staff and less budget allocation in most states in the Northeast. After getting elected to form the government in 2014 at the Centre, the Modi-led government initiated policy reforms and the launch of many new schemes to positively impact the lives of its citizens. One of the most notable changes in the skill ecosystem was the formation of a new ministry called the Ministry of Skill Development and Entrepreneurship (MSDE) in 2015. India, being the youngest country, had the advantage of having a demographic dividend which could potentially turn into a demographic disaster if the massive young population of India is not skilled and put into the industry for productivity and economic growth of the nation.

Every year, post 2015, there has been an annual assessment and evolution of the National Policy on Skill Development. National skill schemes which started in 2008 as SDI scheme, went on to become Standard Training Assessment and Reward (STAR) in 2013 and Pradhan Mantri Kaushal Vikas Yojana 1.0 (PMKVY 1.0) in 2015. It is now the flagship scheme of the MSDE. The skill initiative under the Ministry of Rural Development earlier known as 'Aajeevika Skill Development Programme (ASDP)' is now known as Deen Dayal Upadhyaya Grameen Kaushalya Yojana (DDU-GKY), which provides free skill training, food, lodging and 100 per cent job placement in the industry. The role of regulatory bodies like National Skill Development Corporation (NSDC), the Sector Skill Councils (SSC) and the National Council for Vocational Education and Training (NCVET) in the Indian skill ecosystem became more crystallized and clear.

The Birth of My Skill-Training Venture

In 2013, I founded my skill-training company, a vocational training and skill development company, with a vision and a passion for equipping the youth with practical skills. The company's journey began with a small team and a big dream—to bridge the gap between the demand of skilled labour and the supply of skilled workers in Manipur.

At the outset, we focussed on providing training in sectors such as hospitality, information technology, soft skills, accounts, electronics and healthcare where job opportunities were on the rise. The company's commitment to quality training and certification quickly gained it a reputation for excellence, setting the foundation for its success.

Our Growth Story

In the backdrop of this robust and supportive skill ecosystem, our firm became the first NSDC funded training partner in 2015 in Northeast India. We became the first training partner in India to work with Power Sector Skill Council and worked in the unbundling of Manipur electricity department into distribution and transmission limited companies and trainings its workforce. In 2017, we dared to explore new territories in the Northeast and ventured outside Manipur to open a training centre in Mizoram, thus paving the way for us to establish operations in other Northeastern states. I am honoured to state that in the last 10 years of operations, our organization has been able to train more than 55,000 young individuals and provided job placement to more than 25,000 youth of Northeast India.

In 2019, we were able to identify adjacencies around our core business of skill-training and we foresaw skills getting integrated with education for employability of the youth. In 2019, we instituted JCRE Global College under Manipur University. In 2020, we established a subsidiatry venture to give captive employment to our trainees, who were trained and certified in the engineering trades. In the same year, a home healthcare company was launched to widen service options in the healthcare. To ease job search for job seekers and talent hunt for the employers, we created Job Xpress, which aspires to become the largest private employment exchange in Northeast India. Our achievements came along with building a strong internal process, a positive work culture, wherein work is executed with ethical practices and adherence to compliances.

The growth story of our skill-training venture has been possible due to the strong shift in skill policy in 2015 initiated by PM Narendra Modi. That led to the fertile ground set for the skill ecosystem to flourish in most Northeast states, which enabled skilling, certification and job placement of the youth in the Northeast. It is heartening to note that a few young individuals were able to earn accolades in WorldSkills Competitions.

The resultant effect of the evolving skill policy is the international labour mobility where the world is looking at India as the skill capital of the world, a country that can supply skilled workforce. There has been standardization of skill recognition between India and many other countries through the signing of the comprehensive Migration and Mobility Partnership Agreement (MMPA). Remarkably, a quantum of this requirement from specific industries around the world is coming to the skilled workforce of the Northeast. Within this context, the global sustainable healthcare system is looking at Northeast India for sourcing of staff in nursing, hospitality, agriculture, construction, and many more, particularly from the United Kingdom (UK), Germany and far-east nations like Japan and South Korea.

Manipur Startup Policy

Northeast India as a region has a huge business potential. The prevailing narrative of Northeast India usually highlights the difficult terrain, geographical isolation, border state mindset, inadequate infrastructure, limited access to finance and market with bureaucratic red tape that makes it difficult for start-ups to grow and scale.

However, in the last 10 years, there has been a lot of progress under Narendra Modi's government, in terms of the ease of doing a business, how a new business could be registered as a start-up which enjoys tax exemption for the first three years, access to fund of funds and other high quality intellectual property services and resources. Most of these steps are digitized as part of the Digital India initiative.

As there are a limited number of government jobs in Manipur, not everybody can aspire for a government job. The only way to create more jobs is to make young individuals become job creators through entrepreneurship. The interesting point to note here is that, the latent enterprising potential of the Manipuri youth is met with the invigorating start-up ecosystem created by CM N. Biren Singh through the Manipur Startup Policy launched on 15 March 2018. The policy is a subsequent effect of PM Modi's strong push on Startup India launched on 16 January 2016. The programme's objective is to empower the youth of Manipur to become job creators by fostering entrepreneurship and developing a culture of innovation, through the most enabling ecosystem to support and nurture start-ups, in order to make Manipur emerge as one of the top start-up destinations in the Northeast.

The Government of Manipur envisages addressing the aspirations of the youth and proposes to strengthen the start-up ecosystem with appropriate incubation and mentoring infrastructure, fast-tracking statutory support and networking of appropriate funding mechanisms. Manipur Technical University (MTU) and Dhanamanjuri University (DMU) are such state sponsored incubators and accelerators.

Some of the notable start-ups under Startup Manipur are focussed on healthcare; processed food created out of local indigenous food; digital leisure and entertainment; AI-assisted reading technology for visually impaired people; digital health platform; block chain and IOT-assisted agri-tech; chocolate; cosmetics; bio-tech companies; tourism; and many more.

The Manipur government offer support to start-ups which are in different stages of the start-up cycle. There are:

1) **Idea stage:** Offers a grant of ₹3 lakh alongside business incubation for innovative and scalable ideas.
2) **Revenue stage:** Provides an opportunity for existing entrepreneurs to scale up their business with financial assistance of up to ₹100 lakhs, inclusive of a 30 per cent grant.
3) **CMESS stage:** Extends support to micro-entrepreneurs by granting a financial assistance of 30 per cent subsidy on the project cost.
4) **Stand up stage:** Focusses on deprived sections of Scheduled Castes (SCs), Scheduled Tribes (STs), and Other Backward Classes (OBCs), minority and women for new projects.

In November 2022, the Manipur state government introduced the venture capital fund for Manipur Startup 2.0 in collaboration with North Eastern Development Finance Corporation Ltd (NEDFi).

Start-up Ecosystem

While our skill-training venture is one of a kind in Manipur's start-up landscape, it is not alone. The state's entrepreneurial ecosystem has witnessed significant growth, thanks to a combination of factors:

1. **Government Initiatives**: The Government of Manipur has been proactive in nurturing the start-up ecosystem initiatives such as financial support, incubation centres and mentorship programmes that have provided a conducive environment for young entrepreneurs. Startup Manipur has been a successful continuing programme in its version 3.0.

2. **Skilled Workforce and MSME**: Manipur has a pool of talented and ambitious youth eager to explore opportunities in entrepreneurship. The availability of a skilled workforce has encouraged the growth of start-ups in various sectors, which resulted in the highest number of MSME registration in the Northeast with 50 per cent of the registration coming from women entrepreneurs of the state.
3. **Improved Infrastructure:** The state has seen improvements in infrastructure, including better connectivity and access to reliable power supply and internet, which are vital for the success of tech-based start-ups.
4. **Supportive Community:** A sense of community and collaboration among entrepreneurs and start-up founders in Manipur has fostered an environment of mutual support and learning.

Impact on the Economy

The success of our venture and the burgeoning start-up ecosystem in Manipur have had a positive impact on the state's economy:

1. **Job Creation**: Our skill-training venture alone has trained more than 55,000 and placed more than 25,000 young individuals in various industries, significantly reducing the unemployment rate in the state.
2. **Economic Diversification:** The emergence of start-ups across sectors like healthcare, agriculture, e-commerce, Information technology (IT), food processing and tourism has diversified the state's economy beyond traditional sectors.
3. **Attracting Investment:** The success stories of Manipur-based start-ups have attracted both local and national investment, further fueling economic growth.

4. **Youth and Women Empowerment:** The entrepreneurial culture in Manipur has empowered not only the youth but also the women to take control of their future, fostering a sense of independence and innovation.

The Road Ahead

While Manipur's entrepreneurial journey is commendable, it is not without challenges. Issues like inadequate infrastructure, bureaucratic hurdles and access to capital remain areas of concern. Nevertheless, the government's commitment to addressing these challenges and the determination of local entrepreneurs suggest a promising future.

In conclusion, Manipur's entrepreneurial journey is a beacon of hope, showcasing the transformative power of innovation and entrepreneurship in a region previously marred by economic challenges, unemployment and insurgency. With the continued support of the government and the collective efforts of passionate entrepreneurs, Manipur's start-up ecosystem is set to play a pivotal role in shaping the state's economy for years to come.

Some of the suggestions here will go a long way in developing Manipur and the Northeastern states as a whole:

1. The biodiversity potential of Northeast India's flowers, wild fruits, indigenous food, medicinal plants and herbs can be tapped. The can be linked to international markets to generate income for the local farmers and women self-help groups (SHGs).
2. The above market linkage can be realized only when we have effective logistic clusters in Northeast India with cold storages at railway stations and airports in Guwahati, Imphal and Agartala for cargo planes connecting them to valuable markets in the Middle East.
3. Our national attitude of treating Northeast India from landlocked region to business land corridor connecting

Southeast Asia can be systematically changed as envisioned in India's Act East Policy.

4. There could be a change in our description of Northeast India as border security to an international economic interface for India's next level of growth.
5. A clear foreign policy towards Myanmar can be strategically developed by the Indian government, which influences, supports and develops Myanmar as India's land business corridor to Southeast Asia and far-east.
6. Bangladesh, Bhutan, India, Nepal (BBIN) Motor Vehicles Agreement must be implemented effectively as Bangladesh has become another strategic corridor for the region to trade through road, rail, ports and waterways with the outside world.
7. Last but not the least, development of the Northeast through infrastructure is welcomed. However, infrastructure development has to be accompanied and supported strongly by human resource development through qualitative, world-class education and skill training in Skill Universities.

ACKNOWLEDGEMENTS

The editors are eternally grateful to each of the 23 illustrious contributors to this anthology: Himanta Biswa Sarma, Kiren Rijiju, Pema Khandu, Yanthungo Patton, Gen. V.K. Singh, Baijayant Panda, Tejasvi Surya, Vivek Singh and Rouhin Deb, Raju Bista, Vaibhav Dange, Karma Paljor, Aashish Chandorkar, Dinesh Nandwana, Pradeep Bhandari, Phangnon Konyak, K. Karthikeyen and Uday Wankawala, Tage Rita, Rami N. Desai, Dr Ankita Dutta, Nilutpal Gohain, Alexander Laloo Hek, Dibakar Dutta and Lairenjam Niranjan Singh (mentioned in chronological order of chapters in the book).

The idea of this anthology was first shared with Shri B.L. Santhosh, National Organising General Secretary, BJP in December 2022. His instant support gave a lot of confidence to the editors to immediately embark upon this fascinating journey.

We are also grateful to Pabitra Margherita, Anupam Yadav, Sonam Chombayi, Rakesh Jain, Major Surendra Poonia, Sirish Govardhan, Shehzad Poonawalla, Manoj Pochat, Rash Rungta and Priyang Pandey whose support helped us expedite the project.

We are grateful to Sanjiv Bajaj who shared our passion for this anthology in the initial stages and supported it wholeheartedly.

A special thanks to Kapish Mehra, Managing Director of Rupa Publications for his belief in the book. Gratitude is due to Yamini Chowdhury, Aurodeep Mukherjee and Namrata Sarma from the editing team, the marketing team headed by Vasundhara Raj Baigra and Swar Khosla for the cover design.

We wish to express our gratitude to Union Minister Shri Hardeep Puri and Deputy CM of Maharashtra, Shri Devendra

Fadnavis for their kind blurbs endorsing the book. Last but not the least, we are eternally grateful to BJP National President Shri Jagat Prakash Nadda for writing the foreword to the book.

LIST OF CONTRIBUTORS

Himanta Biswa Sarma is an Indian politician and lawyer who is currently serving as the fifteenth Chief Minister (CM) of Assam since 2021.

Kiren Rijiju is the Union minister for Earth Sciences. Prior to this, he was a Union Minister for Law and Justice. He is a three time Member of Parliament (MP) in Lok Sabha from Arunachal Pradesh.

Pema Khandu is an Indian politician and the CM of Arunachal Pradesh. He is the son of former CM, Dorjee Khandu.

Yanthungo Patton is the Deputy Chief Minister of Nagaland and is the party leader of the Bharatiya Janata Party (BJP) legislators. He is also the BJP Legislature Party (BLP) leader in the State Legislative Assembly.

Gen. V.K. Singh, PVSM, AVSM, YSM, ADC is an Indian politician and a former General in the Indian Army. He is the current minister of state in the Ministry of Road Transport and Highways and Ministry of Civil Aviation.

Baijayant Panda is an Indian politician currently serving as the national vice president and spokesperson of the BJP. He was an MP in the fifteenth and sixteenth Lok Sabha from Kendrapara. He was also an MP in the Rajya Sabha for two terms from 2000–09.

Tejasvi Surya is an Indian politician and lawyer, serving as the MP in the seventeenth Lok Sabha from the BJP, representing the Bangalore South Assembly constituency. He is the president of the Bharatiya Janata Yuva Morcha since 26 September 2020.

Vivek Singh and Rouhin Deb are alumni of Indian Institute of Management (IIM) Shillong. Vivek Singh served as the Officer on Special Duty to the Hon'ble Union Finance Minister of India, Nirmala Sitharaman. Rouhin Deb is the chief economist at the Chief Minister's Secretariat of Assam.

Raju Bista is an MP from Darjeeling and a National Spokesperson of the BJP. He is also the managing director of Surya Roshni Limited.

Vaibhav Dange is a policy expert on infrastructure, governance and management. He is the member of board of governors of IIM Nagpur. He is also an author and curator of Build India TV series.

Karma Paljor is an Indian journalist and former television news anchor. His career as a media professional began in 2001. He has been associated with major news channels like CNN-News18.

Aashish Chandorkar is currently the counsellor at the Permanent Mission of India to the World Trade Organization in Geneva. He took up this role in September 2021. He is also a well-known policy analyst.

Dinesh Nandwana is the founder and managing director of Vakrangee Limited, a technology-driven company centred around building India's largest network of last-mile retail outlets. He has over 30 years of business experience. He has been driving and overseeing the overall business at Vakrangee since its inception in 1990.

Phangnon Konyak is an MP, Rajya Sabha from Nagaland. She is also the State President of BJP Mahila Morcha, Nagaland.

K. Karthikeyen and Uday Wankawala is the CEO of Atal Incubation Centre (AIC) Assam Agricultural University in Jorhat,

Rupa
6917
18/1/25

Assam. Uday Wankawala is the CEO, AIC Rambhau Mhalgi Prabodhini Foundation in Thane, Maharashtra. Both incubators are supported by Atal Innovation Mission (AIM) and NITI Aayog, and are a part of the Atal Innovation Mission fraternity.

Tage Rita is an agricultural engineer and award winning entrepreneur. She is the founder of Naara Aaba kiwi winery in Arunachal Pradesh.

Pradeep Bhandari is a well-known independent journalist, author, political commentator and psephologist. He has authored the book *Modi Mandate 2019: Dispatches from Ground Zero*, an in-depth analysis of the 2019 Lok Sabha election results.

Rami N. Desai is a celebrated anthropologist specialising in the Northeast India. Her research focusses on tribal issues, ethnic identities and insurgency.

Dr Ankita Dutta is a research scholar specializing in Indic and civilizational studies. She is associated with the Centre for Indic Studies at Indus University, Ahmedabad.

Alexander Laloo Hek is a BJP Member of Legislative Assembly (MLA) from Meghalaya and currently the Minister for Animal Husbandry and Fisheries, Government of Meghalaya.

Dibakar Dutta holds the domicile of Tripura and works as an Assistant Editor at OpIndia. He is an alumnus of Ramjas College, University of Delhi.

Nilutpal Gohain is an officer working for the Government of Assam, currently serving as Deputy Registrar of Cooperative Societies. He has authored the book, *The Legend of Lachit Borphukan*.

Lairenjam Niranjan Singh is the Director & CEO, JCRE Skill Solutions, based out of Imphal, Manipur.